"If we as Black women are going to use our courage for anything more, let us use it to facilitate our enlightenment."
NICHOMI HIGGINS, LMFT

PURPOSEFUL PERSPECTIVES

Empowering Black Women Towards Spiritual Alignment, Self-Mastery & Joy

NICHOMI HIGGINS, LMFT

Publishing Services provided by Paper Raven Books

Printed in the United States of America

First Printing, 2021

Paperback ISBN= 978-1-7360258-0-2
Hardback ISBN= 978-1-7360258-1-9

DEDICATION

To my dearest daughter and son, thank you for being the catalysts to my growth. Because of your precious heartbeats, I discovered G-d's love and found myself. I am forever grateful to you and constantly find myself in awe of your beautiful magic. I hope these words always serve as a reminder of your power, influence, and love. To my husband—thank you for being the earth to my water. A man of few words with a heart of gold.

TABLE OF CONTENTS

DISCLAIMER

I've struggled a bit with the layout of this book. While everything covered in these chapters reflects real conversations and experiences discussed in sessions with my clients or lived through in my own life, I will refrain from being too specific to protect the confidentiality of others. However, I am sure you will see parts of your own experience in the examples provided.

Furthermore, throughout this book you will note that I write the name of God as G-d. My parents converted to Judaism when I was growing up, and this was one of the practices that I adopted. The custom of substituting the word "God" with G-d in English is based on the traditional practice in Jewish law of giving G-d's Hebrew name a high degree of respect and reverence. This custom comes from an interpretation of the commandment in Deuteronomy 12:3–4 regarding the destruction of pagan altars. The bulk of Jewish legal opinion agrees that the law only applies to the written name of G-d when written in Hebrew and not when written in other languages. Again, this is my personal preference.

IT ALL BEGINS WITH A DREAM

If we as Black women are going to use our courage for anything more, let us use it to facilitate our enlightenment.
—*Nichomi Higgins*

About a year or two ago and amidst my own process of awakening, I received a dream. I'll go as far as to say that it was the most beautiful dream I've ever had. I should clarify that while I have many dreams, they are rarely memorable. In fact, I literally forget all but a few minor details of my dreams within a few minutes of waking up. But this one was different; life changing even. In this dream, G-d showed me a bright, deep yellow room that held a small audience of people. The room felt charged with energy as people smiled, laughed, and talked amongst themselves.

What initially stood out to me as I surveyed the audience was the lack of diversity. There were men and women; however, I didn't see any faces of color. I found this odd. Then, like playful butterflies in reverence for one another, two beautiful ebony-colored women dressed in jewel-colored harem pants and white tanks entered the room, black hair free and wild. They radiated joy, and I remember feeling deeply connected to their energy.

In the moment of their entrance, I also noticed that the audience grew silent with anticipation, their faces overpowered by the brilliance of their smiles. As the two women settled comfortably onto their cushions at the front of the room, they explained their intention to demonstrate a type of meditation so powerful that it would ultimately induce a deep trance-like state; the audience applauded. I am not sure why, but I found that weird and a little annoying. Still, I was intrigued and comforted. Sitting in front of each other with their legs crossed beneath them, they held hands, closed their eyes, and began to sing a melody so utterly beautiful that I imagine I would have cried had I been awake. I remember thinking, wow!

Then there was a flash of light, and I was swiftly transported to some other dream scenario. My joy was now replaced with sadness. I can't remember where I was whisked off to, but I do remember feeling an intense determination to get back to the women. Fortunately, my wish was granted. Upon my return, it was clear that things were different now. The room that was once bright and energized was now dark, gray, dilapidated, and covered in what looked like soot. It was as if the place and everyone inside of it went up in flames. The silence was thick and the room still. It almost felt as if some time had gone by, possibly even years. Heart pounding, I wondered what had happened. I surveyed the area in confusion. Then I noticed a figure sitting steadfastly in one corner of the room—legs crossed, posture erect, and covered in the ash. She appeared as nothing more than a perfectly preserved statue from Pompeii. I was confused. Where was the other sister? I walked closer and gently touched the figure. My heart was immediately flooded with peace.

I realized that the two women were alive, but now only as one. Locked into a state of transformation, I could hear the soft whispers of their joint meditation. Her body radiating warmth, her energy was calm and centered. I knew then that the joy I had felt earlier in the dream was their anticipation of finally merging and becoming one. Then she turned to me, and with eyes glowing bright red, she whispered, "Help them become one. Help them become whole."

Now awake in my bed, I felt as if everything within me was vibrating. I am not entirely sure what the dilapidated room symbolized, maybe just a retired reality. But I am certain of this—not only did this dream reveal my call to action. These women symbolized unity, transformation, enlightenment, and above all, congruence with one's highest self (and thus, G-d). They also represent you and me.

* * *

Dearest reader, I am so excited that our paths have finally crossed. If you're reading this book, something called to you. Maybe it was the title that piqued your interest. Or a friend's nudging. Maybe it is because you have transitioned to a place in your life in which you recognize that it is time to make some major shifts. Or maybe you are in a season of life in which it feels as though you are being stretched beyond your capacity and could use a new framework to make sense of your experience. Whatever the reasons, I welcome you.

Through these pages, I will offer perspectives about change, growth, and healing that I sincerely hope will aid you in becoming better oriented on your unique path towards the life you so deeply desire to live. Perspectives cultivated through personal experience, as well as years of working with ambitious women of color guided by purpose and driven by vision. Purpose to create, to love, to lead, and to inspire change. These are the stories of women who themselves have desired to become unstuck from the bondage of a mindset that once oppressed their dreams, desires, connections, and voices. Together, we have sifted through false narratives to find their truth. Within those truths, bodies and minds have been healed, hearts have been opened, and joy revealed.

In full transparency, these perspectives are as old as time. There is nothing new or innovative about what I will say. But the "how," I pray, will resonate with you—resonate on a level that ignites several aha! moments. And while the objectives are clear, I must also make clear that this book is rooted in four fundamental truths:

1. To become the woman who you believe is the best version of self. You must be willing to un-become the version of yourself that operates in a faulty narrative that obscures

your clarity and impairs your connection to your highest self.

2. G-d is not some alien entity that exists within an unseen universe. The Divine Source of Life itself flows through your veins and with every beat of your heart.

3. There is power in perspective.

4. You deserve to ask for help.

Take a moment to sit with these statements before reading further. Speak them aloud. How do the words sound and feel? Are you experiencing any other reactions?

I am encouraging this moment of connection, because these statements will be helpful reminders on your wellness journey. A journey that so many of us are embarking on. Through the years, I have held space for so many women and one thing has become glaringly clear: Black women in particular are beginning to lean into a robust conversation about wellness that promotes our emotional, mental, physical, and spiritual health like never before—a conversation that I have come to understand is a Divinely ignited one. It's as if our spirits are being awakened to the possibilities of life beyond the shadows. Or maybe ashes. Beyond the rules that have painted a picture of how we are "supposed to be." With this awakening comes an awareness that "It is Time"—time to relinquish the burden of existing so that others are not threatened by our voices. Time to release the responsibility of picking up the slack. Time to rewrite false narratives that skew our perception of our worth and value. And the time to heal open emotional wounds and traumas both inherited and experienced firsthand. This call to operate from a higher consciousness is so powerful that it is accompanied by a spiritual awakening. One that requires us to become unified, aligned, and ultimately whole. One with ourselves, one with G-d, and one with one another.

So, I hope that this little book of perspectives serves as a sort of journey map on your path to creating a more congruent and harmonious life. Not only will I shed more light on how to navigate the obstacles that will naturally emerge when one chooses growth over stagnation, but I also hope to facilitate a kind of self-reflection that shifts the way that you think about and experience yourself in relation to the things you are attempting to accomplish in your life. Shifts that will allow you to lovingly release the version of yourself locked in a narrative that no longer serves the woman you are becoming. Shifts that will bring more joy and self-acceptance into your life, which will ultimately enhance that beautiful Black girl magic that you so gracefully encapsulate.

Finally, this little book will nurture a conversation about spiritual growth and your ability to achieve clarity through Divine connection. However, this conversation will not be oriented in any one religious faith system. As a deeply spiritual woman, I understand that spirituality can stand very much alone and without a connection to any specific faith system. Through my own process, I have come to know G-d in a profound way. While I will honor the Universe throughout this book in a manner congruent with who I am, it is not intended to condemn you or your faith system. I must also take the opportunity to highlight that throughout this book, I will refer to G-d in other ways, namely as The Divine, The Source, and The Universe.

To facilitate your reading experience, I'd like to offer tips and tools from lessons that I have learned over the years. Tools that can augment your ability to identify and dismantle any attitudes or beliefs that have been making it difficult for you to connect to the abundance of possibilities that come with being you. Often, these are the beliefs that question your value and efficacy, or perpetuate anxiety, depression, disordered eating, or any other issue that keeps you from living a more fulfilling life. Beliefs that fuel questions like "What's wrong with me?" or "Am I good enough?" etc. Now, while I am a bit of a free spirit, I won't be asking you to do anything too unusual like bonding with your plants and dancing naked under the stars (although they are great things worth experiencing). However, I do have a couple of requests.

First, please read this book with an open mind. Not merely because it provides practical perspectives and tools that can help you move through life with more certainty (even within periods of uncertainty), but also because it's a helpful way of navigating the discomfort that comes with change and evolution.

Second, please commit to reading this book as a participant and not just a reader. I recommend taking your time. Each chapter will provide you with an opportunity to reflect deeply. Whatever you do, please do not consider this a vacation read.

Finally, I ask that you allow yourself to participate in this book with a vulnerable heart. Feel free to reject what is not for you and let in whatever speaks to your truth, even if it feels uncomfortable. I hope you can use this book in conjunction with your own therapy. As a therapist who has her own therapist, there is nothing like having someone hold space to focus on you.

So, fellow travelers whom I may never get a chance to meet, for whatever reasons, our paths are intersecting. Understand this: *You were meant to pick up this book because something has been written specifically for you.* I recommend taking your time on your reflections; download the companion journal and let's get deep!

THE STORM IS THE INVITATION

When it seems like the sky is about to collapse, relax, that's just the roof caving in.
—Jarod Kintz

"Nikki, this is not the life that I imagined; something is missing. While I am grateful for what I have—my husband, kids, home, career, etc.—I am not enjoying myself. I can't seem to stop eating or crying. Sometimes I only eat once a day. I am so tired and annoyed all the time. My hair is falling out, and I can't go to sleep. Sometimes I just want to hide from everyone. I feel like nothing I do is good enough. Ha! I don't even know who I am supposed to be good enough for anymore. Things feel so robotic, empty. I am stretched beyond my capacity. I don't think I can take it anymore. I am over my job; I want to start my own business, but I am afraid. I can't lose the lifestyle that I've created! What will people think? Ahh, my "professional brand," the thing that keeps me chained to other people's expectations. People who don't even get me. People who only see a version of me. Shit, what would people think if they found out I was struggling like this? I believe I am being called to do more, but I just don't know what that looks like. I mean, at what point does G-d make our purpose clear? Do people really even have ONE purpose? What the hell am I doing here? I should be able to figure this out. Why can't I figure this out? I am just ready for my days to feel less like a fight, less like the same damn day every day. I want to feel better about myself and what I have to offer. Ugh, you probably think I am crazy. I am not usually this crazy! AM I GOING CRAZY? Can you help?"

There are moments in our lives when we find ourselves at a crossroads, afraid, confused, and without a road map. The choices we make in those moments can define our futures. Of course, when faced with the unknown, most of us would rather simply turn around and go back. Some of us, in fact, do! But then there are the lot of us that recognize we've come too far to go backward.

The above is a compilation of statements that I have heard many women share over the years. Amazing women—women who work hard, serve hard, love hard, and dream big. Mothers, daughters, wives, and partners. Women who have reached a point in their lives in which they are being forced to recognize that the familiar ways of solving life's challenges have run their course. While this is not the first time that these women have had to navigate adversity, something feels different this go-around. They feel both simultaneously aroused towards something more significant and, for lack of a better word, stuck! Stuck in careers that no longer inspire them or relationships that fail to satisfy them. Or stuck in a problematic way of thinking and doing that is taking a toll on their confidence and connection to self. The result is a life that feels mundane, lacking, and exhausting—an experience that feels much like a thunderous storm of uncertainty. A storm that is nothing short of a real wake-up call.

This is important to note because as Black women, we have been groomed to "rise above"—be strong, wise, and all-knowing. Naturally, when we face the reality that we have reached a point in our lives where the answers are not accessible, this can deeply threaten the integrity of our identities. We ask ourselves, "What do I have to do to move forward?" and consequently, we reprimand ourselves for not knowing. This lack of clarity can invoke a slew of difficult emotions and thoughts for a woman driven by passion. Fear and the fullness of being overwhelmed may fuel thoughts of defeat and self-doubt. Feelings of confusion, anger, and/or sadness create breeding grounds for self-criticism: "How did I get here when I thought I was doing all the right things?" or "What's wrong with me?" This internal exchange, this experience, only worsens our clarity, deepens our fear, and heightens our reactivity to life's curveballs.

I can relate. I've been there—a few times, actually. There was a time in my life when anything that threatened my momentum threatened my sense of self. In fact, I can recall a time in my life when I was so enthralled in exceeding others' expectations by way of success in my career and my relationships that I had become disconnected from myself—so disconnected that I couldn't even remember my favorite color. I remember thinking, "Where did I go wrong?" But I managed (like most of us do) to push through this time in my life. I did my "soul-searching," and even emerged from that situation determined to become a therapist, only to find myself back in the storm many years later! I was so stuck this time that living life itself felt like a battle. No one knew, of course. My pain was my own to hide. In my professional life, my avatar showed up in the world saying and doing all of the positive things that had come to be associated with Nichomi. In my personal life, I was a tired mother and wife. Inside, I felt angry. I thought to myself, "How the hell did I get here again?" and "Why can't I just be fucking happy?!" At this particular juncture in my life, I didn't realize that while I had grown, much of my growth process was impaired because I was desperately trying to keep one foot in the familiar. In other words, my growth was hindered by my limited tolerance for discomfort. Have you ever been there? Eager to grow, but at your own pace and as comfortably as possible? Additionally, I did not realize that each time I found myself stuck, I was being extended an invitation to walk a path that would lead me back home to me. How could I have known? Each storm felt like a personal attack, an endless reminder of my shortcomings. With no end in sight I often found myself fighting for control and relief by any means necessary. The experience was and is altogether disorienting.

That is why I have chosen to begin with this first perspective. It is, in my opinion, the cornerstone of wellness and evolution and often where we wrestle most. As I have mentioned, there is and will always be power in one's perspective. So, I think it is necessary that I place emphasis on the fact that the storm serves as an invitation. An invitation to become aware of your cognitive dissonance and thus incongruence with your Higher Self. As well as an invitation to reconnect to G-d on a deeper more meaningful level that allows you to define a valued direction that leads to your authentic joy. Allow me to unpack it for ya!

The Invitation to Become Aware

To help explain this a little more, I'll share a story:

> *There was a lion that grew up in a flock of sheep, and so he had no consciousness that he was a lion. He would bleat like a sheep,*

he'd eat grass like a sheep. In essence, the lion had become a sheep by association. One hot day, the shepherd who attended the flock sat on a rock taking refuge in the slight shade of a leafless tree. He watched over his flock as they waded into the quiet, flowing water of a river to drink. The lion that thought he was a sheep followed them into the water to drink as well.

Suddenly, just across the river, there appeared out of the thick jungle bush a large beast that the lion cub had never seen before. The sheep panicked, and as if under the spell of some survival instinct, leaped out of the water and dashed in the direction of the farm. Strangely, the lion cub did too!

While the flock scrambled for the safety of the farm, the beast made a sound that shook the forest. When he lifted his head above the tall grass, the shepherd could see that the beast held the lifeless body of a lamb from the flock in his blood-drenched mouth.

Seven days passed without further incident, and then, while the flock grazed, the young lion went down to the river to drink. As *he bent over the water, he suddenly panicked and ran wildly toward the farmhouse for safety. The sheep did not run and wondered why he had, while the lion wondered why the sheep had not run, since he had seen the beast again. After a while, the young lion slowly went back to the flock and then to the water to drink again.*

Once more, he saw the beast and froze in panic. It was his own reflection in the water. While he tried to understand what he was seeing, the beast suddenly appeared out of the jungle once more.

The flock dashed with breakneck speed toward the farmhouse, but before the young lion could move, the beast stepped in the water toward him and made that deafening sound that filled the forest. For a moment, the young lion felt that his life was about to end. He realized that he saw not just one beast, but two—one in the water and one before his eyes.

His head was spinning with confusion as the beast came within 10 feet of him, growling at him face-to-face with frightening power in a way that seemed to say to it, "Try it, and come and follow me."

As fear gripped the young lion, he decided to try to appease the beast by making the same sound. However, the only noise that came from his gaping jaws was the sound of a sheep. The beast responded with an even louder burst that seemed to say, "Try it again."

After seven or eight attempts, the young lion suddenly heard himself make the same sound as the beast. He also felt stirrings in his body and feelings that he had never known before. It was as if he was experiencing a total transformation in mind, body, and spirit.

Suddenly, there stood in the river of life two beasts growling at and to each other. Then the shepherd saw something he would never forget. As the beastly sounds filled the forest for miles around, the big beast stopped, turned his back on the young lion, and started toward the forest. Then he paused and looked at the young lion one more time and growled, as if to ask, "Are you coming?"

The young lion knew what the gesture meant and suddenly realized that he had a decision before him—he would have to choose whether to continue to live life as a sheep or to be the self he had just discovered. He knew that to become his true self, he would have to give up the safe, secure, predictable, and simple life of the farm and enter the frightening, wild, untamed, unpredictable, dangerous life of the jungle. It was a day to reckon with himself and leave the false image of another life behind. It was an invitation to a sheep to become the king of the jungle. <u>Most importantly, it was an invitation for the body of a lion to possess the spirit of a lion.</u>

After looking back and forth at the farm and the jungle a few times, the young lion turned his back on the farm and the sheep with whom he had lived for years, and he followed the beast into the forest to become who he always had been—a lion king.

* * *

My mother first introduced me to this story when I was a kid. I started to experience depression at 11 years old and it wreaked all sorts of havoc on my self-esteem. In the hopes that I would see my real strength and potential, my mom shared this little fable—a powerful example of incongruence that I have referenced many times over the years. However, only recently I began to look at it from a different angle.

The moment at which the lion sees his reflection is a pivotal one, and not merely because he is exposed to his true form. It is a significant moment because he is exposed to the utter incongruence of his nature and thus self. This, my friend, is the source of that stuck feeling in your storm of WTFs!

You are at the crossroads of a Divinely orchestrated wake-up call designed to show you that the life you are attempting to create, or rather, the mindset through which you are creating said life is out of alignment, in some way or another, with your unique and powerful design. If congruence is the attainable state of existing in agreement (or in harmony) with your highest self and your highest power, then incongruence is the complete opposite. Incongruence is coaching self-acceptance and lacking it for yourself. It is practicing forgiveness towards others while holding every mistake over your own head. It is dutifully building others up and tearing yourself down. It is saying that you trust G-d, but never relinquishing control. It is showing up as a lion, talking like a lion, and walking like a lion, only to stare into the mirror at night and see a sheep. This is not an attempt to throw shade, no ma'am. However, it is no secret that in this day and age, it is much easier to look the part than actually live it. I am simply saying that we have all experienced our lives in ways that have greatly contributed to how we make sense of others and our world. More importantly, these experiences (whether traumatic or not) have also become influential to how we make sense of ourselves and ultimately believe we have to "show up." For example, consider the below quote from the work of Mr. W.E.B. Du Bois:

> It is a peculiar sensation, this double-consciousness, this sense of always looking at one's self through the eyes of others, of measuring one's soul by the tape of a world that looks on in amused contempt and pity. One ever feels his twoness—an American, a Negro; two souls, two thoughts, two unreconciled strivings; two warring ideals in one dark body, whose dogged strength alone keeps it from being torn asunder.

I think it is safe to say that being a Black woman in America is not an experience absent of persecution. For example, in order to avoid being labeled angry or aggressive, Black women must create avatars. There is me in the form of my truest expression, and then there is the version of "me" that has been deemed "palatable" by societal standards. This version makes others feel most comfortable in my presence. This avatar comes with job security and career growth, but results in generations of women raised to navigate a world by walking a dichotomous tightrope between being powerfully silent, proudly selfless, and nonthreateningly exceptional. I don't know if that's a word; but you get what I am saying. The endless wrestling with questions like: who do I need to be today, versus who am I allowed to be, versus who do I want to become can sometimes feel opposing, suffocating and again disorienting. While this is not an experience exclusive only to Black women. It is safe to say that we are frankly, tired of attempting to love, create, and lead through these fragmented identities. Because to present as a lion and exist mentally as anything else produces an incongruence that opens our spirits up to depression, low self-esteem, self-doubt, Imposter Syndrome, and anxiety, leaving us to cope. We then find ourselves reverting to behaviors that further perpetuate the incongruence and amplify fear.

How on earth can we walk confidently in our callings if we question whether or not we even have what it takes to produce that which we are being called to bring into the world? How can we find our loving partners if we have not invested the time and energy into truly falling in love with ourselves? How can we fully optimize our presence in new spaces if we question our deservingness to even be included in those spaces?

When you are operating as a congruent woman, you are not looking for pleasure. You are not avoiding pain. You are not seeking approval or admiration. You are no longer bound to or defined by the problems in your past. You are not in competition with others, nor are you governed by their expectations. You are naturally and spontaneously living as a genuine human being. This is the version of alignment that we are called to create from, love from, and ultimately serve from. It simply means that you embrace all of you, your mistakes, flaws, hopes, and dreams. When walking congruently, the world does not define you, because you have embraced your Divine responsibility to define you! It is in congruence that we feel more confident in our ability to follow G-d's plan for our lives without question. Take a moment to imagine achieving your goals through this way of being. If, for a brief moment, you questioned whether or not this state of being is, in fact, attainable, you are not alone; many of us do.

In the midst of this stormy experience—it is difficult to know where to go next. As we all know, being exposed to our own incongruence and knowing exactly where we have become incongruent—or even what to do with that information—are overwhelming experiences in and of themselves. I always say, awareness without action is not enough to move you forward. This is why you must also receive in the invitation the opportunity to orient your steps through the process of defining G-d and then naming your valued direction.

The Invitation to Define and Name

He who has a why to live for, can bear with almost any how.
—Viktor Frankl

If you have not had an opportunity to access the companion journal, now is a good time to do so. After you read this particular chapter, I am going to ask that you spend some time completing the reflection activities in the companion journal, which are designed to increase your awareness and application of the perspectives contained herein.

While illuminating your valued direction requires you to understand where you are stuck, as well as create a big picture of what it is that you want this big ole life of yours to encompass, it must begin with your definition of G-d. Now, I'd like to clarify that when I say "define G-d," what I am actually encouraging you to do is define what G-d means and symbolizes in your life. For example, I personally define G-d as love, kindness, leadership, service, knowledge, beauty, courage, presence, life, hope, and so much more. This awareness influences the values that I choose to pursue and operate within daily. It impacts my business's very infrastructure and my presence as a wife, mother, and friend. If I believe G-d is kindness and courage, then as an extension of Spirit, I must work to exemplify those values in my daily life. I must also seek out the people and environments that allow me to operate accordingly.

So often our definition and understanding are based on what we have been taught through the lens of someone else's interpretation. I hear women everyday enter my office under the pretense that G-d is somehow ashamed of them for not "getting it together." But this is always an assumption rooted in their own self-criticism, an assumption that makes navigating this storm and change feel that much more daunting and lonely.

This particular responsibility is also critical to establishing perspective around the conversation of purpose and self-mastery. I remember sitting down with a good friend, who in the midst of her own storm declared that she had started to question the whole idea of purpose; specifically, whether or not she had one. Turmoil tends to lend itself to questioning everything. Even the things you were once pretty certain of, so I wasn't surprised. However, if you are someone that has found yourself wrestling with the question of whether or not you have a purpose, I want to challenge you head-on and ask that you stop doing yourself the disservice of spending your time entertaining the thought. In fact, I will share with you what I shared with her. First, not understanding or knowing your purpose doesn't mean that it doesn't exist. Second, purpose does not have to be defined by a successful career or business! The idea of one's "unique purpose" is multifaceted and ever evolving. While I believe that I am walking in my calling as a facilitator of change, I have come to accept that I will understand the totality of my purpose when my life nears its end. So, my prayer is that I am afforded the opportunity to do so thoughtfully in old age. Finally, I belong to the school of thought that subscribes to the belief that our ultimate purpose in this life is to seek G-d in all things, including ourselves.

This fundamental pursuit can be initiated or re-oriented in naming your valued direction. I use the term "valued direction" because in addition to defining G-d, it involves clarifying your values and reflecting on what matters to you in all areas of your life. It also includes:

- Reflecting on what you want to stand for in life.

- Revisiting your strengths and areas of needed development.

- Determining how you want to treat yourself and others in the process of living.

Oftentimes, we attach ourselves—and our ability to be happy—to specific ideals or images of success and health, only to find ourselves feeling like failures when those outcomes are not achieved.

So, a valued direction is not a goal or destination, per se. It is more like a path shaped by your values that encompasses your goals. This is a critical point of view that I'd like to share because many people approach values pretty traditionally, i.e., "I value family, love, hard work, etc." Since most of what we understand about our value system is inherited—and frankly, a little undercooked—it is not uncommon for people to lose track of them entirely or otherwise struggle to consciously integrate them into their lives or businesses. Consider your value system as more than just a list of words, but as an essential tool—a compass, to be exact! This compass's function is to move you towards your valued direction and assist in both your decision-making and your ability to present more congruently in your life. You see, when you are aware of what you value in life, you are less likely to find yourself lost in depression or anxiety. Lost in fruitless relationships or careers and lost in debilitating confusion and self-doubt. Your lack of awareness in this area is the number one indicator that you are out of alignment, and thus walking on your path with impaired judgment. That feeling of purposelessness that you experience from time to time—well, Sis, that is G-d's way of showing you that you're not using your compass!

Now, when we can accept that even when we don't have a full understanding of our purpose, at a minimum, our ultimate purpose is to define what G-d means to us, we can then allow this robust definition to shape our values. From there on we must intentionally choose to use those values as our compass daily. Not only do we begin to move out of feeling stuck, but we open ourselves up to the most authentic version of ourselves. We open ourselves up to aligning with our highest selves. We open ourselves up to transformative change and possibility. In this shifting and becoming unstuck, we open ourselves up to the regular instruction of G-d and what it truly means to be purpose-driven and purpose-FULL.

Now, imagine what shifts could happen today if you became more familiar with what mattered to you and decided today to begin living accordingly. For example, if you value kindness, how is it demonstrated in your business and leadership philosophy? How is kindness conveyed within your marketing strategy? Better yet, how do you choose to show kindness daily? And I don't just mean towards others, but kindness towards yourself. For example, when I am under the thumb of my own self-criticism for making a mistake, I will stop to ask myself, "Can I speak more kindly to myself in this moment?" I'll admit, speaking to yourself in this way may initially sound cheesy. This kind of self-talk is intentional and requires practice, but consider how you are currently coaching yourself through life. Furthermore, how would the quality of your relationships, career, business, and life change? Would you become an even better human in the process?

Take a moment to sit with all of this. Scan your body from head to toe. Do you notice any tension? If so, where? Why do you think it exists? Or do you notice peace? Take a moment to journal your thoughts.

In the companion journal, you will be able to complete a copy of my valued direction assessment. You can use this activity to set value-congruent goals. You can also use your insights to guide, inspire, and sustain ongoing action. If you don't have an answer to a question, that is perfectly okay. Simply state, "I don't have an answer yet." Every unanswered question will begin to reveal more clarity around what may be contributing to your feeling stuck and the ways in which congruence will bring more enriching value to your life.

There is one important point that I would like to note as you complete your reflections and that is to resist the urge to censor yourself to "adult" all over yourself. You don't have to write pages, but just write down what comes up for you. For some of you, the answers to these questions will be as clear as the bluest sky. For others, it might feel like you've been asked to put together a 500-piece jigsaw puzzle with no picture. I can relate to being in both places throughout my own journey. In fact, in hindsight, I recognize that both were instrumental to my ability to walk within my calling confidently today. We all have an idea of what it is that we want, especially what we want the quality of our lives to feel like. Sometimes it comes out in the form of "if only…" statements, or my personal favorite, "In an ideal world, I would be able to…" We've gotten really good at allowing our responsibilities, past mistakes, and fear to scare us into overthinking and questioning everything, especially about the lives we truly want to manifest—the lives that G-d is allowing us to attain! So, we adapt to the safe and censored version of ourselves, often to the point of disconnection and incongruence. This way of making sense of ourselves in the world can breed a mindset of limitations and skewed perspectives. Try also to avoid:

- Asking others what they think; this is all about you

- Rushing through the activities

- Assuming that you don't need to complete the activities because you already know where you're going

- Giving up when you can't answer the questions

Once you allow yourself to engage this storm from a different point of view—a point of view that affords you an opportunity to find your footing in what matters to you—the question that should naturally emerge is "What do I have to do to begin moving in this direction?"

Like the lion who emerged from the storm understanding his incongruence, your awareness alone is not enough. In order to operate, create, and experience life congruently and in alignment with your highest self, you must lean into the meaningful process of transformational change. This is the process of unbecoming.

Reflection Questions:

- Does it currently feel like you are stuck in the midst of your own personal storm?

- Where specifically are you feeling stuck (e.g., career, relationships, etc.)?

- What shifts can happen today if you became more familiar with what mattered to you and decided today to begin living accordingly?

- Who do you need to become and what do you need to believe in order to live a life of joy?

Feel free to be comprehensive when answering. Consider areas in your career, business, relationships, etc. You don't have to answer why just yet. "Why?" tends to open the door to judgment, and we can spend all of our time judging ourselves and not really getting oriented in the process.

When you are done completing these reflection questions, scan the QR code and complete the valued direction activity in the digital companion journal!

SURRENDERING TO TRANSFORMATIVE CHANGE

For a seed to achieve its greatest expression, it must come completely undone. The shell cracks, its insides come out and everything changes. To someone who doesn't understand growth, it would look like complete destruction.
—*Cynthia Occelli*

If you're willing to allow yourself to accept that you are not under attack; but instead being extended an invitation to grow, you are officially oriented. While the storm may still feel very present, hopefully there is a bit more clarity around what you're moving towards.

Whether you are calling it "evolving," "shifting," or "pivoting," my dear, you are talking about change;

and the topic of change is an interesting one. We all recognize that it is a part of life and even understand that it causes discomfort, yet we dread it daily and continually search for new ways to make it a quicker and convenient process. Unfortunately, our Western society has conditioned us to doubt our innate ability to evolve peacefully through change. Our ability to control as many variables as possible has somehow become the more accurate measure of our efficacy as people. This "change scary, control safe" mentality obscures the fact that change is in fact an anointed process that, while challenging, is the only way to propel you towards advancement and true enlightenment! To experience transformative change is to willingly choose a process that will require thoughtful reflection and intense wrestling with none other than who you are at your core. It is a process that influences the way you move through time and space and a change that liberates your mind and promotes congruence. In fact, I'll go as far to say that pursuing personal congruence through transformative change promises alignment and self-acceptance on a deeper level—a recalibration of sorts. A level that rejects the idea that the total collective experience of inherited rules, traumas, racism, and stereotypes are the only foundation from which we must create our successes. In fact, it is my opinion that transformative change affords us the opportunity to create based on the future we are building and not the past that we are determined to escape.

Having accumulated thousands upon thousands of hours helping people grow over the years, I have been allowed to watch change unfold in a myriad of ways. Combined with my own personal experience, this exposure has not only helped me understand the significant role that spirituality should play in the process of change, but it has allowed me to pull from psychology to construct an explanation of the transformative change process that generally resonates with my clients.

As I see it, change unfolds in three logical phases. This perspective is influenced by the transtheoretical model of change, which posits that people move through a series of stages when modifying their behavior. While the time that a person can stay in each phase is variable, the tasks required to move to the next phase are not. Most of us are familiar with behavioral change. This type of change is rooted in conditioning, i.e., "When I think A and I do B, I'd like to respond in C instead of D." While this sounds straightforward, anyone who has ever made and broken a simple New Year's resolution can appreciate the difficulty of changing our behavior. Making a lasting change in behavior is rarely a simple process. Usually, it involves a substantial commitment of time, effort, and emotion. I love this particular model because it rests on the premise that change is not linear, but cyclical. In other words, until the desired outcome becomes as routine as waking up in the morning to pee, you will move through these phases again and again, progressively learning more and challenging the obstacles that impair full adoption.

Although a helpful framework for organizing my earlier handling and understanding of change, the model insufficiently addressed the simultaneous spiritual awakening that many of my clients were also experiencing. Since transformative change is all about shifting from the idea of "I want to stop doing" to "I want to start being," I decided to create a point of view that better encompassed both the psychological and spiritual experiences that occur. As a result, a more holistic view that embraces the presence of Divine guidance is provided.

Borrowing a bit from the transtheoretical model, I like to conceptualize transformative change as follows:

Phase One: The Storm (aka the Invitation)

I pretty much shared what this phase encompasses in the first chapter. Still, I want to highlight that it is very possible to become overwhelmed with the sense that things are unraveling in your life. As a result, it is not uncommon to fall into unhealthy coping behaviors such as excessive drinking or substance use, overeating (or not eating), shopping, isolating, etc. I think it's fair to say that this storm can be appropriately described as a "damn doozy" because it is often triggered by any of the following experiences:

- Some external events (i.e., divorce, job loss, loss of a cherished relationship, medical diagnosis, etc.)

- A traumatic experience or disaster

- The realization that you've become disconnected from what truly matters to you. Or, that the life you have built and the life you desire to live are out of alignment with what truly matters to you

- Choosing to pursue a dream or passion that pushes you out of your comfort zone (i.e., starting your own business, etc.)

- Choosing to cultivate a personally meaningful relationship with G-d

- Living for years in trauma or with a form of depression and/or anxiety, and finally seeking therapeutic support to resolve it

- G-d's call...period!

It can feel like a complete crisis! In its extreme, my clients (including myself) have experienced symptoms of depression and generalized anxiety. It is not uncommon for people to experience amplified emptiness, loneliness, unhappiness, mental and emotional exhaustion, despondency, and feeling lost or without purpose, synonymous with statements like "I am just so tired of living like this," "I feel as though my spirit is under attack," or "WTF is going on with me?!" The emotional and spiritual turmoil that we experience in this phase can make us feel like we're losing our minds. So much so that random panic attacks, frequent crying spells, mood swings, and irritable outbursts become par for the course. For others, sometimes, the only thing that makes sense is that nothing makes sense.

Since a large part of moving through this experience is shifting your perspective, accepting the invitation to name your valued direction and choosing to embark on the journey represents *real* change. The whole experience can feel like fumbling for a light switch in a pitch-black room. If this is difficult for you to do on your own, chuck that pride out the window and seek professional guidance. A trained professional can help you challenge the fear and negativity that comes with the discomfort of this experience. Again, please rebuke the idea to "go it alone and figure this out by yourself." No one will give you brownie points. In fact, your growth process is more likely to get hijacked without the objective eye of a professional calling out obstacles and setbacks. Besides, this phase only marks the beginning. Accessing support now will help you in the endurance game. While friends are great and their support is valuable, they may not always be able to offer you the space and time that you'll need to peel back the necessary layers—layers that may be contributing to the places where you are feeling stuck. We often chat with our tribes only to get lost in a "me too" conference. Not at all throwing shade, but merely stating that sometimes, you just need a space to process *your* stuff.

While I truly understand that everyone may not have the financial resources to hire a therapist, you can certainly leverage the abundance of information available online (e.g., social media), look into local or broad-based support groups, attend church or worship communities, etc. Wellness is more accessible than you may be allowing yourself to accept. Besides, Black women also have a right to ask for help without feeling like some cardinal rule is being broken.

So, what are specific barriers to navigating the storm effectively?

- Staying stuck in your negative self-talk, the kind that promotes your fear and those icky ideas of you being a disappointment, etc.

- Seeking distractions from the discomfort (i.e., drugs, alcohol, sex, shopping, overemphasis on work, etc.).

- Trying to go it alone. (This is especially important for those of us who pride ourselves on generally helping others figure their ish out. Remember, no brownie points.)

- Comparing yourself to others.

- Classifying this as some sort of punishment because it's uncomfortable.

- Feeling guilty. (Haven't we all experienced the low- and high-key guilt trip merry-go-round?)

Phase Two: Ego Confrontation

Nan-in, a Japanese master during the Meiji era (1868–1912), received a university professor who came to inquire about Zen.

Nan-in served tea. He poured his visitor's cup full, and then kept on pouring. The professor watched the overflow until he no longer could restrain himself.

"It is overfull. No more will go in!" the professor proclaimed.

"Like this cup," Nan-in said, "you are full of your own opinions and speculations. How can I show you Zen unless you first empty your cup?"

While I wish I could tell you that butterflies and rainbows will greet you after the storm, I cannot. But with the help of the tools suggested in previous chapters, you'll be more aware of the process in which you are engaged. In essence, up until this point, you've become awakened to your incongruence. You've shifted your perspective to welcome change rather than despair. You've re-oriented yourself in your understanding of G-d. You've sought out professional guidance and you've gotten oriented in your values (and thus, valued direction). You should be entering that first therapy session, like, here!

In this phase, you are tasked with the responsibility of confronting how you are, in fact, perpetuating the problems in your life. This is the phase in which your faulty beliefs, attitudes, and actions are identified, confronted, and either revised or dismantled altogether. This is where your mind begins the process of becoming unleashed. This is also where resistance and ambivalence will show the hell out. Since this is where much of the wrestling and growing happens, it is also where the most time is spent. By time, I mean months—even years. In all honesty, it has taken me a few years to work through my ish, and I am pretty positive that there is still a bit more that I am working through—remember, the journey is cyclical. Please don't get scared! While the transformation process can feel painful and disturbing at first, this is also the phase in which life begins to take on new meaning. You will have moments of clarity, growth, and understanding that are, for lack of a better word, amazing! I launched my business in this phase, I lost weight and healed my body in this phase, etc. Again, it may sound cliché, but there is always a silver lining in the midst of any storm. Keep going. Keep moving forward.

Consider it this way. If that little lion, seeing his reflection in the river, is the wake-up call, then actually learning to accept and live like a lion is the phase of ego confrontation, because it involves recalibrating the very narrative through which you operate. So, don't go getting any big ideas, you high achiever! There are no shortcuts, as this good work is by no means a sprint. Allow me to put on my therapist hat for a moment.

Think of your operating narrative as a collection of beliefs or assumptions that have been formulated and reinforced over time through personal experiences (good, bad, and ugly); inherited lessons (e.g., the Black girl code of conduct); sociocultural rules, expectations, and ideals; and messages from friends, family, etc. This narrative begins to form the minute you enter the world and develops deep roots as you grow throughout time. Your ego is shaped from this narrative.

In the world of psychology, the ego is our sense of self, or "I." When you say things like,

- "I am [your name]."

- "I have a [job, house, car, mother, father, spouse, child, headache]."

- "I think [insert a thought]."

you are operating from your ego. The ego is possessive because it experiences itself as separate from everything else. So, your operating narrative shapes how your ego pursues your most basic human needs: physiological needs, safety needs, need for love and connection, esteem, etc.

These beliefs or assumptions aren't all bad. However, some are particularly problematic because they are the products of difficult experiences that may have gone unprocessed—often consciously and/or unconsciously suppressed. Beliefs such as, "I am not good enough" or "I only matter when I am succeeding" ultimately influence the lens through which you make sense of yourself, others, and the world. These assumptions also determine your fears and the ways in which you choose to operate with respect to the things you fear.

For example, because of my depression and low self-esteem growing up, I became a person with a "type A" personality that struggled with perfectionism in my professional life. Job performance was my barometer. Let me be clear, I did not resolve the depression or low-self-esteem. I just figured out how to look like I did. I guess I needed to make up for all of that time feeling like a shitty and inadequate person. My ability to meet and exceed the high expectations of others was rewarding and contributed greatly to my professional success, until it eventually left me drained, depressed, and almost void of my creative energy.

I have also had clients who, in childhood, had to assume the roles and responsibilities of a caregiver, resulting in "parentification." Not being able to simply be a kid is certainly problematic. But the bigger issue that all generally report is the fact that no one seemed bothered that they were asking these children to take on adult roles and responsibilities. It was an expectation, a norm even. What frustrated my clients the most was the fact that when they would make a mistake or do a job incompletely, they were reprimanded like adults. "You should have known better," "How could you let that happen?" or "Get over it" are inherited and invalidating messages that they still repeat to themselves today. These same women also adopted a belief at a young age that they are only valuable when doing for others. The consequence? Unnecessary and predatory pressure and fear! Pressure to do everything right and fear of being abandoned or judged when making a mistake.

As a result, we ego-driven humans do what humans will always do—we take those assumptions and we create rules. Rules to protect and rules to optimize our survival and overall sustainability. I like to call these "self-governing rules." Common examples of self-governing rules and some related self-talk include:

- Be kind and courteous to others; when they go low, we go high…sigh.

- If you're going to speak, have something meaningful to say.

- Keep your expectations of others low (to avoid disappointment).

- Don't get too sad or angry, you'll lose control.

- Don't let people see you cry; they'll mistake your meekness for weakness.

- If you want people to like you, put their needs first; take care of others before taking care of yourself.

- Be the best in everything that you do; you can't afford to be basic.

- Mistakes make you look weak; "we" don't get second chances.

Now I want to be clear in saying that these rules can get dark and even toxic, depending on the experiences that shaped them. But like our beliefs, all of our rules aren't problematic, nor are they permanent fixtures in our minds.

In fact (and fortunately for us), there is also the higher self, which is not driven by our basic human needs. Instead, our higher selves are calm, neutral, compassionate, understanding, and intuitive.

While the ego accumulates knowledge through learning, the higher-self intuits reality by virtue of what it is. The ego thinks. The higher self knows. The ego exists in your cognitive mind and the higher self in your heart-mind. But up until this point in the change process, we haven't really fooled with or tapped into anybody's higher self. Instead, we identify exclusively with our egos and the beliefs shaped by our operating narratives. While clearly irrational, every negative thought that we think about ourselves looks and feels so believable.

That is why the purpose of transformative change—specifically, this phase of change—is to help you tease out those problematic rules. As women seeking purpose, desiring to create from purpose and love from purpose, it is important to understand how these rules obstruct your clarity and impair your growth, flexibility, and ability to pivot as/when necessary.

So, as the process of confrontation and growth unfolds in phase two, the ego begins to sublimate to the higher self. In the language of Taoism, the lower self gets refined into the higher self. This process may create a sensation that your life doesn't make sense anymore. It is simply the product of having your former beliefs, desires, and paradigms challenged and often disproven—a necessary part of your expansion.

So How Does One Navigate Phase Two?

Remember that in this phase of change, the primary focus will be on exploring how certain beliefs or rules drive the behaviors and attitudes that are keeping you from living more congruently. Since the key to moving through this stage is allowing the simultaneous processes of confronting the ego and learning to trust the higher self to inform new ways of thinking and operating, the extent to which you immerse yourself in the process will significantly influence what you get out of it. To willingly navigate this phase of change is to become more deliberate and intentional. I have had clients stall this effort, for their fear of leaving the comfort and familiarity of their bondage felt far too great. I speak these words not to cast a shadow of shame upon them, but to honor that we all progress at our own paces. However, with each aha! moment comes a revelation of self and understanding of G-d that renews and restores.

I have so many fantastic clients, but let me share the story of one in particular that comes to mind. I remember our very first consultation. She said, "Nikki, there are some things I need to release, and I need to know that you are the woman to help me do just that!" In this particular conversation, Lisa (name has been changed for the purposes of this book) explained that she had already been working with a therapist, but the work wasn't happening at the frequency or pace that she desired. She wanted to dive deeper—it was time. She was also working in an environment that triggered her issues surrounding abandonment. Her boss, another Black woman, managed her team through her own insecurities, resulting in a professional culture of criticism, micromanagement, and punishment. Let me tell you that Lisa showed up to every single therapy session with pen and journal in hand, ready to work! She would come to sessions with notes she had taken from sermons that she had listened to, books she had read, and reflections that produced insights. When I gave her a list of feelings to reference in our work, she didn't just reference it, she studied it. This level of commitment to self simply blew my mind. But she isn't the only one. The clients who typically get the best results from their process of change are the ones who do the work. Such women put family and friends on notice, stating, "Y'all, I am in the process of growth, so some things about me are going to look and feel different!" These clients are also willing to learn how to tolerate the discomfort—another important component of effectively navigating this phase of change.

The heart of transformation is not only about action; it is also about mindset. Discomfort is inevitable. Stumbling will happen throughout the process. Reverting back to old behaviors will occur. Fear is unavoidable, but as we already know, not all of these things have to be wrong. I think we can all agree that there are some big, beautiful, sparkly words and phrases out there like "glow up, level up, shift, pivot, and manifest"—powerful words being wielded by people who are doing the work, and by others who have only learned the language. Like Benita Butrell from *In Living Color*, "I ain't one to gossip, so you ain't heard it from me!" but I can say that anyone who is really doing the work learns that it is tough to manifest from an incongruent sense of self, no matter how specific you get in naming that which you desire to manifest. It also becomes clear really quickly that the destination that is your best self is always one step ahead. One minute you're glowing, and the next minute you're growing, and growth ain't always glamorous. I have been navigating my own transformational path for nearly four years now, and I am absolutely in love with the woman that I have become in the process. My initial experience in phase two was a doozy, but I survived. Don't get me wrong, my life is not absent of adversity but I have a whole new armory to reference. This is why support will always be a necessary part of the process. If you've been thinking about getting a therapist, take this as a sign of confirmation. Now is the time!

Finally, to make it through phase two, you will need to become a practitioner of you! This means that you will have to prioritize you without asking for permission! I haven't even published this book yet, and I felt someone roll their eyes! During a talk that I led, I remember being asked by an audience member how putting herself before others is an act of a G-dly woman. Now, mind you, this was a group of businesswomen coming together to discuss ways to better manage stress and burnout. They wanted to know the secret to better career-life balance. Each desired to be in a space that promoted their personal growth and wellness. These women were passionately pursuing their purpose through their businesses, caring for their families, serving within their communities, etc. Each also collectively agreed that they often felt tired and overwhelmed and felt a great sense of pressure "to be and do all the things" exceptionally well. However, this particular woman was very bothered by my words. So much so that she came for me with scripture!

This is not the first time that I have seen a raised eyebrow in response to this prompt. So, after validating her concern and settling the nerves of my inner feminist, I stepped into my wise mind and asked the following questions: "Have you ever wondered why women are groomed to honor G-d through service to others and men through manifesting His vision? Better yet, how easy has it been to hear the voice of G-d when meeting the needs and expectations of others? What energy reserves are you allowing G-d to actually work with?" I am assuming that these questions struck a chord because she nodded her head in understanding and shared her thoughts.

Later that day, I remember thinking to myself, why does the idea of putting ourselves first still conjure up feelings of neglect, selfishness, and irresponsibility? I imagine that the answer to this question will look different for each of you. Even if the idea of taking an entire month away from our responsibilities seems ideal, this is not necessarily what it means to prioritize you. Rather, prioritizing you merely means reorienting your connection to self, to G-d, and to what matters to you. It is also asking, at what point is my service to others more about my need to feel loved than to serve G-d?

I want to make a brief comment here about the first question that I asked this audience member about how men and women are groomed. I want to reiterate that the Universe will further enlighten your understanding of G-d and the word you access G-d's teachings through within this change process.

Phase Three: Harmony in Existence (aka the Phase of the Lotus)

This is the phase in which you begin to exist and operate according to your new self-awareness. It is about maintenance and integration. This is the phase in which you perform, function, build, and create as one with your highest self, and thus G-d. We'll explore more in Perspective #10. In the interim, know that it exists.

Because change unfolds in a progressive cycle, I want to be careful not to use finite words like "destination" and "arrive." The truth is that when you say yes to this kind of change, you have committed to the constant yet peaceful pursuit of your best self. As you progress on your path, the first and second phases will feel less disruptive when you revisit them. This has a lot to do with the fact that you are more aware of what is happening and more in sync with both your higher self and higher power.

In sum, remember that change is disruptive and detoxifying. It requires us to note the strengths, weaknesses, and comfort areas that breathe life into our fear of discomfort. It demands that we choose what we will leave behind and what we will bring forward into the new. Change is the voice that asks, "Do you still need that, or has it served its purpose?" Let's be real, human beings are collectors of things, people, and experiences. The idea of letting go or leaving something or someone behind to create space for a new and unpredictable experience can provoke worry and fear, and that is okay. But you can't cut corners or speed up the process. Transformative change is a process that takes time and one that has no firm destination. If you allow yourself to surrender to the process of change, then you can accept that you will always be in pursuit of your better self until you rest your precious head. Since discomfort will manifest itself, so will growth and the spiritual awakening that coincides with it. Because when we undergo transformative change, we are literally learning to change the lens through which we evaluate everything, including ourselves. Beliefs, habits, and social (as well as familial) conditioning will be questioned. Life is evolution, and change is merely a simplified term used to describe that process, so denying ourselves evolution due to our own comfort is denying the very composition and function of our existence. That resistance can result in sleepless nights, self-doubt, depression, and so much more. More often than not, change refines our resilience, and resilience is the gift of life that keeps giving. Whether you're leading a company, community, your family, or just yourself, lead to build resilience through an increased openness to change. But to be clear, resistance is also a pivotal part of the process, which we'll explore deeper through the next perspective.

Reflection Questions:

- Take a moment to consider the last time you might have experienced ambivalence. What did you have to do to move through it? Or are you still stuck in it now?

- What are some things that you have told yourself in the past to participate in change?

- What scares you about changing? What excites you?

CHANGE COMES WITH RESISTANCE

No matter how much she accomplished, she never felt like it was enough. So I asked, what is standing in your way? She replied, "Well me, dammit!"
—Nichomi Higgins

To paint a proper picture of resistance, I'd like to start off with a little transparency. Writing this book has kicked my Black girl, magical ass! For years, I have wanted to write a book, and for years I found myself uninspired to do so. I figured that when the moment was right, it would reveal itself. When the moment finally arrived, and the desire to write was placed upon my heart, it was as if everything in my spirit had been ignited with excitement. When accompanied by a big idea, I have somehow come to associate this emotional combination as a message from G-d. Historically, I've been right, but I can admit that I have not always interpreted the instructions correctly. Actually, let me be even more honest—I have often interpreted the instructions wrong...a lot! So, when I received this Divine order, my gung-ho ass sprang into action! I was going to write a book about fear for women of color determined to start and/or run their own businesses. After all, I had been running a successful practice at the time, so a book about business mindset seemed pretty straightforward.

Admittedly, it was also December of 2019. The excitement that comes with leaving a year behind and stepping into a new one was charged with excitement. We were all striving to "glow up," "blow up," and win! Many people, including myself, had proclaimed 2020 as the year to take things to the next level. Every business coach held the blueprint to success and six figures. Every psychotherapist wanted to help you become a better version of yourself. I wasn't any different—I wanted to contribute to that conversation too, but something felt undercooked for me. I felt off. I chalked it up to a little writer's block, and in my usual determination, I set my sights on writing a kick-ass book. I totally wish I could insert that little emoji of the woman holding her head, because if G-d were a Black mother, I am pretty sure She was yelling, "Girl, sit down and wait a minute! I haven't told you everything yet." What can I say? I can be such an eager beaver!

High on my homemade cocktail of arrogance and optimism, I entered 2020 with two thousand whole words on a digital page and immediately hit my first wall. Something was missing. I was supposed to be writing about fear, mindset, and business, but the words weren't coming. My inspiration felt muted. Still, I trudged along this writing path for weeks. I attempted to meditate my way through my creative blocks. However, clarity never seemed to present itself, only fragmented ideas that I struggled to cohesively interpret. I was growing annoyed. I remember thinking, "this is all starting to feel much bigger than me," so I hired a writing coach assuming that would be the solution to my problem. Little did I know this problem had some real depth to it.

More words on a page and then WHAM! It's March of 2020, and the world enters into a global pandemic. Not only were our lives flipped upside down, but our world was also steeped in uncertainty and fear. My brain resembled a barren lake bed. Everything was changing right before my eyes, and I was trying to make sense of it. The world was starting to feel unfamiliar. The word "normal" took on an entirely different shape. Aside from being forced to hide our faces, hide in our homes, and fear one another, we were also forced to sit with ourselves, our pain, our joy, and the results of our choices. Like so many, every part of my life was unfolding within the confines of my home. There was nowhere to run. Nowhere to hide. No way to avoid it. Just when I thought that those walls were closing in further, our world went alight with rage! More Black lives had been taken from this earth with the regard that one might give an insect. It's as if Black Americans felt the collective silent cry of our ancestors in the matter of a few weeks. The sadness was profound. The cries became louder and echoed globally. The pain was intense—the trauma strangely old and yet all too familiar. The exhaustion was heavy, and the anger became both consuming and overwhelming. We had no more storage space. Some of us short-circuited and exploded, while others became numb. I wanted and needed to cease all of my efforts and properly process my thoughts, emotions, and feelings unapologetically. I didn't want to talk. I just wanted to be, to exist in my own space and sort through the minutiae of what was happening to my community, giving myself a chance to reflect in real time. I wanted to write and yet I struggled to translate my thoughts into readable words on a page. This carried on for months, ya'll.

In this fog, I began to second-guess everything, including myself! The exhaustion mounted; the goal felt unattainable.... I wondered, "why was doing the thing that I knew I had been called to do being met with so much damn RESISTANCE?" What was I missing, not seeing, or unconsciously rejecting? Then in one of my intense "why the hell am I writing this book again" crying sessions, I realized I wasn't being honest with myself. My fear of failing, being judged, and letting you down was influencing my subconscious decision to write the book I thought was safe and not the book I knew Spirit was instructing me to write—a book that focused on change, spirituality, and self-acceptance. From that moment onwards, this book evolved and became its own journey. Now, with newfound focus, I released my need to write under the influence of my fear. I now understood that G-d was using this process to reveal my voice in a new medium. Although scary, I was now more driven by my curiosity.

If the term resistance within the context of growth is unfamiliar, I'd like you to consider the last time you exercised or engaged in any strenuous activity. Typically, when you begin any workout, you will start with a goal in mind; even if that goal is simply "lawd, please don't let me pass out!" As your body engages the workout, you'll begin to feel tired, possibly winded, and maybe even experience some pain. This discomfort leads you to check in with yourself, or it may lead you to question your will altogether. You may ask yourself questions like, How much longer do I have to do this? or, Can I endure more of this? This, my friend, is an example of resistance described in its simplest form!

Still, I'd like you to store it in your mind as the energy of opposition. It is synonymous with change, evolution, and the pursuit of one's purpose, so there is no way around it. Its primary function is to test your will, distract and expose you to your perceived limitations—emphasis on "perceived." Resistance is activated by one's desire to lead, achieve, heal, and become "more than." It is not inherently evil, but as Steven Pressfield beautifully proclaims,

> To yield to Resistance deforms our spirit. It stunts us and makes us less than we are and

were born to be. If you believe in G-d (and I do) you must declare Resistance evil, for it prevents us from achieving the life G-d intended when he endowed each of us with our own unique genius.

You see, resistance is self-generated and self-perpetuated. It is the unconscious influence of the mind upon something that it does not yet fully embrace or understand. Imagine standing at the base of a tall, beautiful mountain. Everything in you can already imagine what life will be like at the top, because you know you're supposed to be there. Still, you find yourself a little overwhelmed with thoughts like, How am I going to get up there? Is the top really where I want to be? Why can't I be there already? or Do I even have what it takes? Here's the deal: The entire idea of the mountain is an illusion created by resistance. As much as we outwardly maintain that we would like to improve our lives, we only allow ourselves to move forward incrementally. Again, a lot of this has to do with the fact that we have been conditioned to associate change with uncertainty. However, it also has a lot to do with fear and we'll talk more about that shortly.

The key things to note about resistance is that it can be an indication that you are operating in fear or out of alignment with what really matters to you. However, its presence can also be a symbol that you are moving in the right direction. A good friend pointed out that in addition to my fear, the resistance I experienced in writing this book was the product of my impatience and my ego. I was so focused on being perceived as the expert, that I overlooked the fact that writing this book was just as much about my growth as it is about being a resource for yours. Had I allowed myself to be more patient with myself and the process, I might have had an entirely different experience, perhaps an experience of more flow and ease. I'd also like you to note that when it surfaces, it can present itself in many forms, often within the following three categories:

Conscious and Obvious: Ambivalence, for example, is the experience of wanting two opposing things with the same intensity. For example, have you ever found yourself wanting to grab drinks with friends and also lie nestled in your cozy bed? You spend all day going back and forth in your head only to finally make the decision to meet friends. However, the comfort of your bed won and now you're running 45 minutes late and catching all the side-eye! Not only are you perceived as a procrastinator, your time management is also under question. When this behavior is applied to the consideration of change, our ambivalence is demonstrated in the desire to both grow and stay in the familiar. Resistance leverages ambivalence as a tool to feed on our inner fears and delay our growth (regardless of how much). In fact, ambivalence can suspend change altogether. Fear, doubt, perfectionism, and procrastination are other forms of resistance perpetuated by our fear-based internal self-talk, which we will unpack later in this book. Thus, it is important to recognize that the very presence of ambivalence is a direct indication that you are indeed wrestling with resistance.

Unconscious and Less Obvious: Going through creative blocks, having a scatterbrain, and/or being on the perpetual hamster wheel of "DOING, DOING, and more DOING" are common examples found within this category. Here, we notice that our steps are not congruent with the direction needed to bring life to our dreams. Notably, fear can also present in this category—the fears of letting others down, leaving folks behind, etc.

External: Resistance that comes from the outside world can show up in the form of those pesky surprises or obstacles that keep popping up in your life and feel a lot like setbacks. While life will be life, these external macro and/or micro challenges might feel like tests or triggers.

Now, here is the deal: All of us are worthy of success when we take responsibility as the creative directors of our lives through change. But we must accept that resistance comes with the territory, even when we are doing what we believe is aligned with our purpose. Therefore, the keys to navigating resistance are:

- Anticipating its presence. In practice, this looks like asking the questions: "How would I like to maintain alignment or access optimism, confidence, or support in the face of opposition today? Especially when that opposition is created by me whether knowingly or unknowingly." This is also a great prompt for meditation sessions.

- Identify which category of resistance you may be experiencing. The goal here is all about taking action to address or rather confront the mindset driving the resistance behaviors. For example, I had a client who felt overextended in her business and also stuck. Her exhaustion turned into doubt, overwhelm, and irritability, which ultimately translated into an intense battle with frequent panic attacks. Using questions that I have included in this chapter and a fear activity that I have included in the companion journal, we could see that a lot of her resistance was stemming from the unconscious category. She was stuck in a work hard, not smart cycle. Ultimately, she built her business on the idea that she had to earn the right to charge more money, call herself an expert, etc. Unfortunately, this way of operating depleted her energy and left her in the position of always questioning her value. When you question your value, you also struggle to assert firm boundaries. When you don't have firm boundaries, it is easy to feel a lack of security and a heightened sense of "what will people think if...." With awareness established, the business of shifting out of that mindset had to commence.

- Consciously pushing through fear on our journey towards purpose.

- Seek spiritual attunement. We'll be covering this next.

When navigated effectively, the outcome will always result in a fortified mind and spirit.

Reflection Questions:

- Take a moment to reflect on an area of your life in which you might be experiencing resistance in relation to your valued direction. What kind of resistance do you experience (e.g., procrastination, distractions, self-doubt, etc.)? How does it stop or stall your actions?

- What actions have you taken in the past to push through?

- What areas in your life do you believe resistance presents the most? Why do you think this is the case?

- Now that you know what resistance is, what actions would you like take to take to push through it when it presents.

Remember if your struggling to answer these questions, enlist support from a therapist or coach!

SEEK SPIRITUAL ATTUNEMENT

*The eye through which I see God is the same eye
through which God sees me; my eye and God's eye are
one eye, one seeing, one knowing, one love.*
—*Meister Eckhart,* Sermons of Meister Eckhart

It's 8 AM and the "Sunday blues" have already set in.
Although awake, I am tired, sluggish even. Not in the
mood to be bothered, I decide to shower in my kids'
bathroom. They have a door, and it locks; this is the
only way to guarantee a quiet shower in peace. The
warmth of the water feels like a fuzzy blanket. For
a moment, I think about getting back in bed, and
then, as if my body has been hijacked, I freeze.

*"I am not pleased with you. I have answered your
prayers. I have protected you. I have been waiting for*

you, and yet you do not heed my call. I need you now. It is time. If you continue on this path, it will only lead to more sadness and loss."

For so long, my greatest fear in life was being considered a disappointment. As the eldest child of teen parents, there was a lot of pressure to be a leader and, above all, not to repeat their mistakes.

I spent so many years striving towards being my best so that I might avoid this reality, only to find myself standing butt naked in my shower, overwhelmed by G-d's disappointment and truth. I remember dropping to my knees and crying. It's hard to put the power of that moment into words; it is still with me. My shoulders were buckling under the weight of my accountability. It was as if something deep within me hit play, and scenes from my life started to flash before my eyes. I was being forced to see, and I realized that I was in a one-way relationship, and I was the guilty party. G-d showed up for me daily, and I was always either running late to the date or otherwise, "too busy" to show up altogether. I prayed before every meal, or when I needed a sign or solution. But none of this constituted my right to claim a mutually invested relationship.

Leading up to what I jokingly call my anointed shower, I felt so lost, disconnected, unfulfilled, and unhappy. I cannot deny that I knew G-d was calling me to make significant mental, emotional, and spiritual changes in my life. Changes that would require me to step out on faith and run my business full-time. Changes that would require me to become more spiritually attuned. Don't get me wrong, I wanted to make these changes. But then there was that part of me that would scream, "Seriously! You're never satisfied! You'll never be satisfied! You're so ungrateful! Why can't you get your shit together and make it all work?!" Why couldn't I? I had worked so hard to amass the success that I had acquired, and I was afraid of abandoning it all. I wanted more time to prove to the world that I was far from being a disappointment, and climbing the corporate ladder was the easiest way to get that point across. I had the job title that afforded me "a seat at the table," the influence, the car, and the house. Those things symbolized value—my value. I cared more about how the world perceived me than I did about how the Creator of existence itself might see me. I needed to know that I was good enough, and I told myself that more success was the only way to know that for certain. I was so afraid of what people would think, so afraid of failing. I'm not sure how or why, but I came to believe that I could only trust myself within the framework of being and doing what the world expected of me. I didn't trust myself to interpret G-d's voice, let alone call properly, and the fear of getting life wrong was too great. So, I would ask for one sign after another. As the signs mounted in favor of G-d's will, I still asked for more. I was like, "Maybe I didn't interpret that last one correctly. Send me another please." Y'all, I was literally praying up problems in the form of spiritual signs! I wasn't ready to make those changes—or as I perceived them, sacrifices—so I hid, I avoided; I numbed in the form of drinking every single night. But nothing seemed to work. My body, my marriage, and my children were all paying the price for ego and my conscious resistance.

But in that moment of experiencing G-d's voice, I was shown my truth. In one singular moment, nothing felt familiar, and everything felt charged. The Universe had revealed my incongruence and my calling in one fell swoop. With tears in my eyes and truth in my hands, the timing was perfect. The Universe had posed the question, "How much longer are we going to do it your way?" I didn't have an answer this time. Humbled, I accepted the invitation to become attuned to G-d's will.

In following my own divinely ordered instruction, I must take a moment within this space to discuss the role of attunement on your path towards your valued direction. You may be wondering how attunement differs from congruence. While subtle, the difference rests on the fact that attunement is the reactiveness that we have to another person; in this case our reactiveness to G-d. It is the process by which we form relationships. Personal congruence on the other hand is the experience of existing in alignment with our values, higher-selves and thus G-d. Within the context of spirituality, attunement is awareness and response to the Divine's instruction. As I have mentioned, when you pursue congruence with your highest self, it is not uncommon to experience a greater sense of self-mastery and a simultaneous spiritual awakening to the depths of G-d's presence in your life.

Some common and often uncommon signs may appear when one is not spiritually attuned. For example:

1. **Unsettling emptiness.** You're busy! You're successful! And you're also feeling unfulfilled. Does it feel like you're living on autopilot and going through the motions? Something

is missing, but you can't quite put your finger on it. You have a deep longing to make a different or more significant impact in the world. Still, somewhere along the way, you lost sight of what that "more significant impact" looks and feels like.

2. **You attach your value to money and things.** Don't get me wrong, assert your value and get your coin! But if you are putting your heart into making money instead of making money as a result of doing something that you love, you're probably feeling stuck. Why? Because when we attach our happiness to cash—which is fleeting—we essentially create limitations for ourselves. Do you think Madam C. J. Walker and Steve Jobs put their hearts into just making money?

3. **Overwhelming fear or worry.** Does your fear of failing or getting it wrong continually require you to attempt controlling as many variables in your life as possible? If yes is the answer, my friend, you lack trust in something greater. In most cases, you're operating with the world on your shoulders,

and you're petrified that one little mistake will send it crashing down. When we explore the various manifestations of fear, it is important to note that an incongruent spirit will result in amplified fear.

4. **Your relationship with G-d is more of an insurance policy.** You are out here negotiating with G-d. You serve out of duty rather than choice and you don't think you're good enough to stand before G-d. Chile, I can go on...

If You Are Someone That Does Not Subscribe to a Particular Religion

I always say that if you can believe in something greater than you, life's obstacles won't feel more significant than you. Your understanding or openness to understanding what spirituality means to you will be a helpful asset in the battle to get you out of your own way, especially as it relates to how your belief system helps you achieve clarity in times of uncertainty.

In my opinion, spirituality is our sense of connection to something greater than ourselves. It is an appreciation for life and all things that contain life. It is a conscious and deliberate pursuit to walk and create from purpose. It is our practice of connecting to our source of strength, kindness, and gratitude daily. Or as John Lennon has so beautifully stated:

> I believe in God, but not as one thing, not as an old man in the sky. I believe that what people call God is something in all of us. I believe that what Jesus and Mohammed and Buddha and all the rest said was right. It's just that the translations have gone wrong.

I didn't always think this way, though. My parents introduced me to the concept of spirituality at the age of 14. At the time, they were in the process of converting to Judaism from Christianity after years of prayer, study, and grappling with what it meant to become Black Jews. We were the kind of family that loved to debate and talk about G-d. My sister and I were never encouraged to remember scriptures, but rather to think about G-d in a much broader way than the words offered in the Bible. However, this exploration was always done within the context of

Christianity. So, when my dad's spiritual awakening led him to convert, rather than deciding for my younger sister and me, my parents asked us whether or not we wanted to do the same. They understood the backlash that came with the choice, because they were living it. However, they also wanted us to understand the power of choice and the responsibility of connecting to G-d accordingly. My sister and I chose neither and decided to be seekers. Now that does not mean that we became atheists. It merely means that we decided to develop our understanding of G-d outside of the parameters given to us. Unfortunately, this was often met with criticism by others who perceived this seeking as risky. I remember my nana sitting my sister and me down one day and dutifully attempting to rescue us from this great sin that we were committing. I explained to my nana that I was confident with my choice, and she looked me square in the eye and stated, "Well, Nikki, you're just going to have to go to hell; but I can still save your sister." I knew at that moment that I didn't want to serve G-d simply because I was afraid of hell. I wanted to serve G-d out of pure love and choice.

Through my growth process, I have come to experience such love. I meditate more than I drink water. For me, active and inactive meditation is a state of mindfulness that allows me to be fully present in my life. Prayer, however, is a very sacred time that I spend consulting with G-d. Meditation allows me to be present to G-d's instruction, even in session with a client. My spiritual belief system has become one that accepts that G-d is more accessible than I have allowed myself to believe in the past— more accessible than a glass of water. I also read tarot, practice Reiki, and believe in the healing energy of crystals. These practices connect me to my ancestral roots and their methods of connecting to G-d. I remember a client asking me, "How do you get your word if you don't read the Bible?" I explained that I read the Bible, study the Torah, and value greatly other sacred spiritual texts. For me, however, G-d goes by many names: "The Divine," "The Source," "Spirit," "The Universe," and finally, "Adonai." Thus, connecting to what feels natural to you spiritually is one of the first steps to tapping into the Divine within. Although each of us may have a different path, the journey to self through attunement remains the ultimate destination.

If You Are Someone That Does Subscribe to a Particular Religion

Here is what I feel compelled to share. If you are in the midst of your storm, I have a strong feeling that G-d wants to have a different kind of relationship with you. Maybe the way that you have constructed the image of G-d in your life needs some revision because you've become disconnected. I meet so many people who say that they believe in G-d but only interact with G-d in church and in times of need, and I meet women who have been taught about G-d through the lens of judgment, fear, and punishment, resulting in a belief system that promotes shame or fear when they make mistakes. Through their pain (or various other reasons), I also meet women who have become angry with G-d (or at least their current understanding of G-d) and have not been able to process that anger because the very foundation of their beliefs was never truly rooted spiritually.

Then there are the women who know that G-d is working in their lives and need help learning how to trust and surrender to the plan. Some of you have been shown who you are to become. However, you are hesitant to move in that direction because you are focused on what others might think of you, afraid of failing or, worse, succeeding! You may also be operating under the impression that you've got time. Please note, the Universe will find a way to bring to light the thing it has deemed worthy. If you won't be the one to bring it into the world, someone else will. Now, I'm not casting stones, because I had my rights read to me in the damn shower! I am just saying, the toughest pill I have had to digest is the reality that I am not the only healer in this world that G-d is calling to serve in this and various other capacities. If I am not up to the task, someone else is and I sometimes someone else has to be. I could go on for days but I won't, because the point that I am trying to make here is that if change is an anointed process, then the pursuit of spiritual attunement with one's Higher-Power must be handled with reverence.

To properly unleash your vision, you'll need to create space for the Universe to begin to reveal itself to you. The how can look different for everyone. I am still growing in this area; however, I can share two notable things that you should try to avoid in doing this work. The first is assuming that your relationship with G-d is good just the way it is. The second is attempting to enter into a game of negotiating in an effort to avoid your discomfort.

You can however, go on a negativity fast, and I am not talking about food. Turn off the volume on anything in your life that does not promote positivity and healing, and begin to consume positive podcasts, books, scriptures, films, etc.—anything that will connect you to hope. Now, this gets difficult when the negativity is coming from friends, partners, and employers. If this is the case, surprise! The result of your incongruence is starting to reveal itself. Still, if you can take a break from friends during your positivity fast, great! Use this time to strengthen your spiritual frequency.

Sometimes, as a result of our spiritual incongruence, we also forget how to pray, so I wrote this prayer one evening for a client, and I hope that it can bring you comfort and clarity. My recommendation is that you start your mornings reading it:

Dear Divine, I know that I am being shaped for more; however, I am tired and afraid. My heart is heavy. I feel lost. I am struggling to find my fight. I do not know what you have in store for me, so I seek your guidance and support in THIS moment.

Please grant me the strength to endure this journey of evolution. Please bring with this growth a renewed sense of self and clarity.

Please continue to allow your love for me to manifest through friendship and support. Above all, please guide me in releasing those beliefs that hold me in bondage to a version of myself that operates in fear and doubt. A version that only sees my inadequacies.

At this moment, I am present. At this moment, I am cared for. At this moment, I am yours. Aśe.

Another way to promote this work is to cultivate a relationship with your Highest-Self.

Reflection Questions:

- Do you feel/sense spiritual incongruence in your life? If so, which sign speaks/resonates with you most?

- Do you find yourself shedding or seeking to shed negative energy unconsciously or consciously?

- How do you define your connection to G-d? What is your daily spiritual practice?

- Have you explored/experienced non-traditional spiritual modalities? If so, which ones do you connect with most?

- If you trusted G-d even more than you do today; how could your life improve? What would it take to move in this direction?

Note: The Purposeful Perspectives: Self-Mastery card deck is a great tool to reference on your attunement journey!

EMBRACING YOUR HIGHEST SELF

*The divine self is the author of our life story, but
without sufficient spiritual awareness the human self
tends to rearrange the plot.*
—*Anthon St. Maarten*

I remember back in 2013 when Kanye West began
to refer to himself as "Yeezus" and released the track
"I Am a G-d." With lyrics that declared he was
a G-d enjoying ménages and massages, it wasn't
surprising that anyone who considered themselves
mildly religious clutched their proverbial pearls and
wondered where he found the audacity to draw such
a conclusion. He was accused of being arrogant and
blasphemous, and some even questioned his sanity.
While a bit off-putting, I'll admit, I found the idea
intriguing and worthy of reflection and exploration.

Like Alice tumbling down the rabbit hole, I stumbled into a new world that further expanded my understanding of spirituality—the Kabbalah. Specifically, it teaches that when the soul comes into the world, it forgets who it is and who it is a part of. As a result, we begin to think, speak, and behave in ways that do not reflect our authentic selves as expressions of Divine energy. The Talmud teaches that we are so powerful that we, like G-d, could create worlds. However, our low actions stifle and hinder our ability to connect to our potential. Heck, I even read passages in the Bible that corroborated the idea that we are the sons and daughters of the most high and thus reflections of G-d's greatness. Apparently, Kanye wasn't so crazy after all!

Then, I stumbled across articles written about our responsibility and purpose as human beings to pursue alignment with the highest version of ourselves. Something about this conversation struck a chord in my spirit that forced me to lean in. I was both fascinated and perplexed Would I ever be able to become "this" kind of self-actualized person? Based on where I was standing in my life, the idea (while intriguing) seemed intimidating.

Namely, it was intimidating because I attached deterring assumptions to it. I assumed that this was an achievement best experienced in old age or wealth. I allowed myself to believe that I would have to live life like a monk. I even told myself that the whole idea was "too New Age." I mean, what would I look like as a Black woman talking about operating in my highest self? Would I come off too "holier than thou"? How would people make sense of me? It wasn't a language that was common to most Black folks then. I mean, it was not too difficult to picture my mother's raised eyebrow and pursed lips in response. These assumptions and my loyalty to a false narrative limited my perception of who I could genuinely become at that moment and, ultimately, led me to move on from my research. In hindsight, I realize now that it just wasn't time. I wasn't open.

Defining the Higher Self

Up to this point, I have briefly defined and referenced the higher self while placing deliberate emphasis on your pursuit of congruence. You may be wondering why. Well, it is only in our pursuit of our own congruence and harmony that our highest self is allowed to emerge in our lives.

In the Ifá religion, one's higher self is called the Ori or Ori-orun, meaning both divine mind and destiny. It is the aspect of you that shares its heavenly consciousness with Supreme Consciousness. It is the wise being within. It is a guide that helps you see characteristics that impede your growth and aids you in decision-making. This optimal version of self is the source from which your ability to forgive, hope, and love spring forth. It is the version of you that longs to fulfill your purpose and desires to hear G-d's call. Your higher self knows you far better than you can know yourself, simply because it is the totality of all of your selves: past, present, and future.

Let's make this concept more applicable to life. In matters relating to love and connection, operating in our highest self provides us with a foundation of self-love and compassion that affords us the courage to assert our individual needs and boundaries without internal scrutiny and criticism. Our capacity to understand forgiveness and acceptance is increased so that we may practice both towards ourselves and others without feeling as though we are sacrificing our integrity. In other words, my ability to practice acceptance does not mean that I am giving the undesirable thing permission to continue to wreak havoc in my life. It means that I can accept its existence regardless of whether or not I want it to be there. Being aligned in our highest selves amplifies our ability to choose and cultivate more meaningful relationships because it guides our pursuits towards our valued directions. Unique connections can be formed in your adult life that feeds your spirit in ways that surprise you! For all of my single ladies reading this book, while being aligned does not diminish the desire to find a loving partner, it also allows you to be more patient and confident as you wait for the right partner to be revealed. Your highest self will push against the desire to settle or compromise those qualities and characteristics that are most important to you. It will also greatly influence the lens through which you define your partner.

As it relates to our professional aspirations, regardless of whom we aspire to become or what we desire to create, it is important to remember that our lives' purposes are to use our transformations to help transform our respective environments. In deeply exploring our divinity and purposeful gifts, we can find the guidance and resources to bring to life the most extraordinary of dreams. Remember, within this authentic version of self, your full potential in life can be realized. In business, alignment with your highest self will allow you to lead, advocate, create, and influence more confidently and virtuously from your strengths with fluidity.

While everyone's experience of engaging with their higher self will be their own to metabolize, I can confirm that you do not have to join a monastery to access and exist within this version of self, because it has been with you since your first breath. I am confident that you have experienced your higher self from time to time in the form of your intuition. However, as you learn to explore and TRUST yourself more deeply (which I hope this book will allow), you will gradually uncover your real power and gifts. This realization will allow you to better find meaning in your past failures, mistakes, and hurts. This is when you begin to believe in yourself again while simultaneously becoming powerful beyond measure. Over time, this level of attunement is what I hope to help both my clients and you lovely readers to attain. Whether in business, relationships, or life in general, it is beyond possible to exist, create, succeed, and influence in alignment with your true self, your G-dly self.

Creating Space for This Relationship to Emerge

Meditation and Prayer

There's a reason why these are first on the list: Meditation allows you to silence your thoughts and reach new spiritual heights through your very own breath and stillness. Prayer will enable you to engage in active consultation with your higher power. We often go into prayer asking for so much that we forget to actually stop and listen for the answer. Meditation allows us to exist in our spiritual selves. To practice, start with just five minutes a day and gradually build yourself up to longer meditation sessions when you're ready. Try to avoid judging yourself. The practice of meditation is learning to be comfortable in a state of active stillness. It takes time and looks different for everyone. You can meditate anytime, anywhere, like on a walk or at your desk. At the end of the day it is all about your intention. I generally encourage my clients to set the clock for five minutes and use that time to check in with themselves using the questions shared below to help facilitate the dialogue within:

- What am I grateful for? (Always start in gratitude.)

- How am I feeling right now?

- Is there anything that I need?

- What are my intentions for the day?

If your meditation challenges have more to do with finding a space, don't rule out your closet or a park.

Allow Kindness to Be Your Guide

Many people operate on the frequencies of fear and scarcity. In turn, we see war, starvation, crime, struggle, arguing, and all sorts of other disasters on both large and small scales. However, if we all tuned into our divine nature and realized that kindness is the essence of life, this entire world would function so differently. If you want to embody your highest self, give yourself subtle reminders throughout the day. Examples include: "I can be kind to myself" or "I can be kind to others" or "Is this the best, kindest choice I can make for myself?"

Try to let kindness be a key catalyst for all of your words, thoughts, and actions. With practice, your energy will shift over time, and each step forward makes tapping into your higher-self achievable.

Now, I know that this may sound weird, especially if you have a history of being hurt or taken advantage of. I can honestly relate, as kindness has been the remedy to my lifelong battle with depression. When I allowed myself to embrace kindness, rather than love or forgiveness, hope and healing became more accessible realities that I could experience. Let's be clear: I live my life through the lens of kindness. However, I didn't have to compromise my strength to do so—full stop! Kindness has allowed me to advocate for and assert myself and my boundaries more succinctly in any situation. It has also allowed me to challenge how I speak to myself during moments of incongruence.

Follow Your Own Heart When Making Decisions

This might seem presumptuous, but at the end of the day you know yourself better than anyone else. If you don't feel happy in your current job, seek a new one on your own terms. If you hate the city you live in, move somewhere that aligns more with your interests and lifestyle, even if your family and friends don't agree with your choice.

To honor your highest self, you need to follow your own heart so you can become the extraordinary being you were meant to be. You can't expect a flower to bloom in the wrong climate, and the same applies to you.

Now I will say the greatest roadblock to practicing this skill regularly is trust. More specifically, our ability to trust our true selves. Not only have we been conditioned in our western society not to make heart-based decisions, we tend to hold grudges against ourselves. It's as if every mistake that we have made is recorded and used against us, which results in a fear or hesitance to make decisions and take risks.

One of my bestest sister fiends (this is not a typo) decided that she was going to up and move her children to Costa Rica. She had been talking about it for years, and finally she just said, "I am doing it." While I knew I was going to miss her, I admired her ability to take the leap. Further in this book, we will explore what makes this particular skill difficult on a larger scale.

Speak to Your Higher Self Daily

Even if the communication is only one way initially, request your higher self's guidance and wisdom to vibrate higher throughout your day. You might start seeing strange synchronicities through songs on the radio, repeating numbers on the clock, vivid dreams that seem very real, or even meeting people that you feel you have known forever. Your higher self wants to contact you after a long hiatus, but apply patience and remember that he or she will speak to you when you're truly ready to listen. Answers will come when you least expect them, but please note that the answers will generally be direct. Give yourself grace when doing this work.

Avoid Labeling Your Emotions, and Watch Your Words

"Words are seeds that do more than blow around. They land in our hearts and not the ground. Be careful what you plant and careful what you say. You might have to eat what you planted one day." I am not sure who said this, but it strikes a chord of truth. Two of the modalities that I often reference in therapy are acceptance and commitment therapy (ACT), as well as Narrative Therapy. Both are modalities centered on the premise that reality is given meaning through language.

By perpetually fighting emotions and viewing the uncomfortable ones as "bad," you will only invite them to come back with even more vengeance the next time around. The key is to understand that emotions are only given meaning by the actions we assign to them. For example, if you lash-out and curse others in your anger, you might come to label your anger as bad. However, the truth is that it is possible to be angry and not lash out. It is important to look at your emotions as teachers; they all have important lessons to convey to you, but you have to keep your ears and mind open to retain the messages. This conscious shift in identifying and then embracing your emotions can look something like, "Sadness continues to enter my life, and I am not sure how to manage it" versus "I am always so sad. I'll never be happy."

Walk the Middle Path

To walk the middle path means replacing "either-or" thinking with collaborative "both-and" thinking. Too often, we make up our minds about how we feel about something using a black-and-white, all-or-nothing decision-making construct. When we do this, we run the risk of swinging out of balance—not giving deserved validation to another way of thinking. When we disagree with someone, it may be natural to believe that they are wrong and that we are right. However, when we're practicing empathy, is that necessarily true? The short answer is no, not necessarily—especially when we take a dialectical approach to our thinking by appreciating and making space for diverse viewpoints to pair with our own perspectives. When we replace "either I'm right or they are right" with "I'm right *and* they are right," then we can see each perspective as an opinion rather than an absolute truth. This is such an aha! moment when learning how to navigate different levels of difficulty in relationships in both our personal and professional lives.

When we walk the middle path, we make room for compromise. When that compromise validates our own feelings and those of another, we are on the path to a more harmonious outcome. Consider the results of extreme thinking. Often, extreme thinking leads to extreme feelings—one becomes either too emotionally invested or "checks out" completely due to frustration. Sometimes extreme thinking causes us to become too rigid or too loose. In other words, we make too much of a situation or too little of it. Conversely, acceptance and change are most readily available when we choose to Walk the Middle Path. In doing so, we become unstuck. We gain flexibility so that we can value our own perspectives in proper balance to the opinions of others, pivoting where necessary. Walking the Middle Path creates the type of open-mindedness that facilitates fairness and respect. Quite simply, it's a powerful mindset for creating peace and contentment.

Spend as Much Time Outdoors as Possible

Have you ever just admired the magnificence of trees up close and personal? What I love most about trees is the idea that each once started from nothing more than a seed. When I feel overwhelmed, I imagine what trees have had to endure to grow over the years. I think about all of the lives one tree has touched. I think about the many functions it has served, and above all, the seasons it has weathered. I do this because I pull strength from this line of questioning and thinking.

When you sit and ground yourself in Mother Earth and become friends with the trees, birds, sun, and earth itself, you will start to remember that you and all other life—regardless of form—are weaved into the same web. To reconnect to such wonder, allow yourself to get lost in nature for the afternoon and just forget about all of your responsibilities for a while.

Our people are people of the land and earth. Our ancestors understood how to coexist with nature and harvest its abundance. However, we have been removed from our natural environment and have lost our close bond and connectivity to nature. For this reason, spending lots of time outdoors can rekindle your ties with the earth and bring about remembrance of your true origins.

As your highest self emerges and becomes more present in your life, it is natural that it feels unfamiliar—foreign even. However, I offer this analogy originally shared by the eminent kabbalist Rav P. S. Berg:

> When we are first becoming acquainted with another person, recognition of that person is based on physical appearance. Lacking any experience with the thoughts and feelings of the new acquaintance, we have no firmly grounded expectations. We may have hopes and fears concerning the new person who has come into our lives, but we do not have trust.

> As time passes and the relationship grows, we begin to know our new friend's mind and heart. We begin to see this person with our spiritual eyes as well as our physical senses. The emotional and spiritual bond

that has formed is not affected by absence because it exists beyond the dimension of physical experience. Our friend's mind and heart remain interwoven with our own, unchanged.

In fact, when people have gotten to know one another very well, whole conversations can take place entirely within their heads. We know what our friend would say if he or she were present, and we can hear it being said in our thoughts.

This is what it will feel like to become acquainted with your highest self. This is what it feels like to evolve.

Reflection Questions:

- Based on the suggestions offered, what actions can you start taking today to create space for your higher-self to emerge?

- What daily actions do you employ to anchor yourself when feeling stressed or disconnected from self?

COMBATTING THE THIEVES OF CHANGE: FEAR & SCARCITY

Our deepest fear is not that we are inadequate. Our deepest fear is that we are powerful beyond measure. It is our light, not our darkness that most frightens us.
—*Marianne Williamson*

Let's start with a few questions to ignite your awareness of the thieves of change. If the forces of fear and self-doubt were neutralized in your life, who would you be free to become? And what would you allow yourself to explore or pursue? When you quiet the outside world just enough to hear yourself think, who do you hear? Is it your voice? Or is it the voices of others' expectations? When you think of the future that you're working so hard to create, who or what is the impetus?

I am sure that you are no stranger to fear. But are you aware of the ways in which it manifests in your life? Are you familiar with the ways in which your identity has become structured around your fears?

In my opinion, there are two kinds of fear. There is the biological fear rooted in the limbic system, responsible for our fight, flight, or freeze response. This is the fear that drives our innate ability to stay alive (or at least, to fight for our lives). Then there is what I call ego-driven fear. Ego-driven fear is also rooted in survival—specifically, our ability to fulfill those basic human needs that I mentioned earlier. It is important to make this distinction because biological fear is innate, and it is generally activated by true and present danger. Ego-driven fear is cultivated and shaped by our operating narratives. *As a result, it is activated when we perceive a threat to our ability to meet our needs or follow those rules.* Consider for a moment the things that activate fear in your life—things like losing a job, making a mistake, being alone, etc.

Once we make the distinction between biological fear and ego-driven fear, it is then important to create space for a conversation around what it means to be a woman, what it means to be Black, and what it means to operate through a lens of scarcity. Steeped in generations of racial and gender discrimination, it is no secret that the collective strength and contributions of Black women are undervalued. It is no secret that our beauty is misunderstood, as is our passion. It is no secret that Black female bodies are over-sexualized, objectified, and taken for granted, resulting in a lack of protection and society's disgraceful rejection of that responsibility under the excuse that we are strong. It is no secret that Black women reflect the highest cases of anxiety and depression. It is no secret that sistahs reflect higher rates of unresolved cases of sexual trauma and abuse—and by unresolved, I mean unprocessed. Despite these apparent truths, it is also no secret that we are in so many ways brilliant, ambitious, resourceful, and so much more. So, it is safe to say that a perspective of scarcity exists within our operating narratives—perspectives inherited from generations of women and men who preceded us. People who had to fight just to get a foot in the door, let alone a seat at the table, or people who did not fight at all. When we take into account the sum total of what we have been taught (both directly and indirectly) as well as what we have personally experienced, we must be open to exploring the ways in which fear manifests and aids in our avoidance.

In fact, allow me to take a brief moment to define avoidant coping. Avoidant coping is any form of coping (healthy or unhealthy) that "feels good in the moment" and allows you to avoid the discomfort that comes with resolving a problem. Some unhealthy examples include overeating, over exercising, under-eating, purging, and excessive shopping, just to name a few. These behaviors are often the product of fear, self-doubt, and even dread. To some extent, we all engage in some level of avoidant coping. However, it is important to note that coping is about employing healthy tools that aid in your healthy *tolerance* of discomfort while you work to resolve the issue. As I have jokingly said to a client, "If the only way to determine whether or not the monster is in the closet is to open the closet, hiding under your bed and deep breathing is not coping, it's avoidance!"

With that said, let's continue on to examine some of the more common covert manifestations of fear:

- Scarcity mindset

- Active avoidance

- Imposter syndrome

- Perfectionism

Scarcity Mindset

Generally discussed within the context of financial wealth and abundance, scarcity mindset, by my definition, is a perspective rooted in the belief that life is full of limitations and hardships, such as limited resources, limited opportunities, limited affection, and limited time. A scarcity mindset is a source of self-doubt that often takes form as that nagging internal voice telling you that who you are, what you have, or what you do is not enough. It is the "I gotta get mine" or the "there's only enough room for one of us" mindset. Naturally, this lens shapes how we treat ourselves and others, how we seek G-d, navigate obstacles, seize opportunities, and experience our ego-driven fears. Because this manifestation of ego-driven fear promotes constant self-evaluation and scrutiny, it also amplifies the need to control even that which is realistically out of our control, thus impairing our ability to allow the revelation of G-d's plan for our lives. So, we high achievers find ourselves tangled in a web of passion, purpose, and fear. Fear of failing and "letting everyone down." Fear of judgment. Fear of surrender. Fear of vulnerability and of taking risks. Fear of not being seen. Fear of being broke. Fear of running out of time. Fear of being perceived as weak or fragile. Fear of being abandoned and alone. Most of all, fear of our authority over ourselves. How dare we manifest who we see ourselves to be?!

In a scarcity state of mind, we become little more than pawns in the game of life. We ask questions like: "Can I really achieve this?" "Am I asking for too much?" "Am I good enough?" "Can I really charge that much?" or "Do I even have a right to be here?" We use our bodies as leverage. We procrastinate and make excuses. We buy the designer bags, shoes, and lace wigs but avoid investing in our mental health or businesses because "the cost just seems a little high." We overestimate the challenges in our lives and underestimate our ability to effectively resolve those problems, resulting in our depression and anxiety. If you didn't catch that, I will say it again—A symptom of both depression and anxiety is the consistent ability to overemphasize the negative aspects of our lives and underestimate our sense of agency to overcome.

A practical example of scarcity is the tendency to try to do everything yourself. This has been the crux of my existence! What can I say? I was born to two amazing, hardworking parents who had me as kids themselves. I watched them build our lives, brick by brick, with very little money. There were times when that government cheese was welcomed, and when those food stamps were a blessing. I remember my 11-year-old self, hopping into the back seat of my dad's old, baby blue, 1968 VW Fastback with my ration of trash bags in hand, ready to go clean a few fancy office buildings well into the night. I remember wanting and being unable to afford the name brand shoes and clothes that my friends had, so around high school, I adopted the mindset of, "if I can't afford it, not only will I just do it myself, but I'll prove to the world that I can do it better." While this was a great way of making it through back then, however, as I transitioned into adulthood, I forgot to revise this rule. I took on the "I can just do it myself attitude" in every aspect of my life. While there are some great benefits that come with getting ish done your way, there are also costs. Not only did I become a jack of all trades and a master of none, but I lost time. I always felt tired, and frankly, some of the results of my efforts were less than satisfactory. For example, I couldn't afford the exact wedding dress that I wanted so I made my own dress. It was pretty, but the fit wasn't ideal. Now every time I look at my wedding photos, I see a happy moment and an ill-fitting dress. It wasn't until my third year of being in business for myself that I realized that there is a time to DIY your life and then there is a time to invest in it. I remember thinking, "I am trying to fulfill my destiny, not prove to the world that I don't need help." I quickly learned that asking for help and having my own therapist and coach(es) were keys to my sanity and the successful implementation of my vision.

Active Avoidance

Another common manifestation of fear is active avoidance.

Does the idea of taking time to be still induce guilt or, worse, anxiety? Do you avoid conflict like the plague? Have you ever said to yourself or someone else that "patience is not your virtue"? Do you yourself feel a sense of duty and obligation to volunteer and contribute your expertise? Does it often feel like you are creating from an empty emotional fuel tank? If the answer to any of these questions is yes, you are not alone! I speak to women every day who share their fear of being patient, still, or paused. So I ask them to consider why they believe they have to do and be ALL the THINGS. For most, it is due to rules hidden in their fear of being left behind, failing, failing others, being forgotten, or worse, losing relevance, value, or importance.

There is a scene in one of my favorite movies, *The Imitation of Life*, in which the character Annie asks her dear friend Lora if her then-famous boyfriend, David (a playwright), will ever slow down. Lora responds, "My dear, Annie. If he does, I am afraid he will realize just how sad he really is." This statement really resonated with me from the first time I heard it. It was as if both actresses paused the television and turned to look at me for a brief moment. Chile, I deeply inhaled and slid a bit further under my covers! Was I an active avoider? The answer was a booming, "Girl, yes!"

Active avoidance is a form of escape that involves taking on responsibilities to avoid facing our fears or to avoid thinking or feeling things that are uncomfortable. It is also a way of coping that I am sure all women, but especially high achievers and women of color, have been conditioned to employ in the face of discomfort and uncertainty. While we build monuments of success, we drive disconnection from ourselves and others. We "push through" and further perpetuate our fears. I do want to take a moment to emphasize that this is a form of avoidant coping that only becomes problematic when it is employed to avoid confronting deeper issues or concerns within. For example, if you are unhappy in your marriage and choose to increase your time spent at work or take on new projects to minimize contact with your spouse rather than confront the problem, you are engaging in avoidant coping. Please note: I do understand that navigating communication around marital dissatisfaction is difficult, but I hope you're picking up what I am putting down.

In active avoidance, attending to ourselves is an inconvenience. In active avoidance, we fear vulnerability because vulnerability is not only expressing your truth, but it is also being present to see if your truth has been received. But above all else, active avoidance impairs our ability to find our power and thus, G-d's instruction in the pause.

When this form of fear overlaps with scarcity, time becomes our nemesis and serving or pleasing others becomes intricately woven into our measures of worth. We say things like, "I don't have time to sit around talking about my feelings. I have shit to do. I have a business to build or kids to raise, a partner to please, etc." We fill our figurative plates, fearful that if we set boundaries, loved ones will feel unloved or opportunities will be lost forever.

If any of this resonates, take a moment to consider for yourself the catalyst behind this way of being and doing. For me, it was my fear of becoming irrelevant. As a little girl, I didn't really think I had much value because of my depression. However, as I grew older and accomplished more, it felt so good to be recognized for my contributions pursuing that feeling was like a drug. Wherever the bar was set, I wanted to always go higher, above par. The more I succeeded, the more I avoided dealing with the real issue, which was simply the fact that I still believed I had no real value. I believed that I was only important and valuable when I was doing and succeeding.

Perfectionism

Ah, the "P" word. As a self-proclaimed perfectionist in recovery, I always like to explain to my clients that perfectionism can be categorized in two ways. The first is the more familiar way in which the individual must be the best and produce the best in all things. There is no striving in perfectionism, because it is not the journey but the destination that matters. The second form of perfectionism can be demonstrated when a person is so fearful of not succeeding that they'll often avoid the attempt altogether. Same fear, just a different way of approaching it.

Since a lot of perfectionistic tendencies are rooted in fear and insecurity, life becomes narrowly focused on one thing, and that thing is being the best in as many areas of our lives as possible. Either way, in this mode of thinking, you are prone to overanalyze the decisions that you have to make (even when you know the best course of action), and you subject yourself to competition, self-comparison, and a grueling internal voice that never seems quite satisfied with your efforts. In the world of perfectionism, there is always room for improvement—always an opportunity to be and do better; mistakes are perceived as devastating blows to your confidence and image. So, the scarcity fears of "dropping the ball" or "letting others down" become the foundation for your decision-making, often telling yourself, "I've got to be my best, or else…" even if producing the best comes with rigid expectations of self and exhaustion.

You're probably thinking, Nikki, perfectionism is not that bad. You're right! It's not all fire and brimstone. People like the results that perfectionists produce. They follow through, they are high functioning, hardworking, dependable, reliable, and trustworthy. When you're more than just a workhorse, rather a perfect workhorse, you're likely to experience some job security and a lot of people who value your contributions.

So, it's no surprise that our code of conduct requires it. However, people rarely understand the internal conflict experienced when perfectionism becomes your shield and measuring stick. For example, it can be a source of validation and acceptance—a means of establishing authority and control in one's own life—and a way of avoiding judgment and criticism that is common amongst individuals who have a history that includes physical, verbal, and emotional abuse or violence. It can also be an attempt to avoid failure and the perceived consequences, which is common amongst individuals raised within a highly critical/rigid or "success only" home environment. The following figure highlights common statements that signal perfectionism may be running amuck.

Source of Validation & Acceptance	Attempt to Avoid Criticism or Failure	Attempt to Prove Value and Hide Insecurities	Source of Control
Rules/assumptions that accompany these functions			
"I know that if I am perfect, people will like me, respect me, and need me." Or "If I do everything right, people will tell me that I am doing a good job."	"If I say and do the right things and can be the best, I am less likely to experience criticism or rejection."	"My work is a reflection of me, and I want to be perceived as having it together."	"If everything is in place and perfect, then it is under control and manageable."

Whatever the function of your perfectionism, it is so important to understand that perfectionism can become a barrier to the life that you are trying to create because it not only confines relationships, it also limits our relationship with G-d. When we think we have to do everything right, it creates this space where we don't let G-d operate in our lives. Why would we? If we are doing everything right, we shouldn't need the aid of The Divine, right? Cultivating a perfectionist mindset means cultivating a mindset of scarcity that makes self-acceptance a narrow target and failure a wide net. Unfortunately, when your perspective on what is exceptional is inflexible, not only does your internal voice become one of constant self-criticism, but it can spill into how you lead, evaluate, and relate to others.

It also greatly impacts how you connect to your body.

This conversation is not about throwing the baby out with the bathwater. Instead, it is designed to get you to take a moment to reflect on what perfectionism looks like for you. I am sure it has produced much success, but at what cost? Think about your valued direction. Think about what it is that you are trying to achieve in your life. In what areas of your life do you feel the need to perform perfectly? Why? What are the feared consequences when you're not perfect? Now, reflect on your responses and list three ways in which the quality of your life would improve if you could shift this way of being to allow more room for grace and flexibility.

Imposter Syndrome

You are standing on a new stage amongst those who you consider far more accomplished than yourself, and you feel out of place or worse, like a fraud. Who cares that there is actually evidence that you deserve to be there?! If the mysterious "they" only knew the lengths that you go to hide the fact that you feel inferior in your beautiful skin. If they only knew that silence is a time to ruminate on the thing you didn't say, should have said, or didn't say exactly the way you wanted to say it.

Imposter syndrome is a more acceptable way of saying, "I suffer from toxic and chronic self-doubt as it relates specifically to my achievements." Imposter syndrome is when really great people doubt their accomplishments, hard work, or talents; persistently question their worthiness to hold space in certain environments; and fear being exposed as a "fraud." As the birth child of scarcity and perfectionism, imposter syndrome thrives on self-comparison and is a dangerous head trap for a woman who desires to create an authentic and harmonious life aligned in purpose and in congruence with her higher self.

If thinking you're a fraud is a daily monologue and you have recently found yourself stuck, surprise! This is a way of thinking about yourself that only G-d can break. You're not just the lion living as a sheep; instead, you are the lion living as a lion and thinking you're really a sheep! You are living under the radar in hopes that none of the other lions find out that you are a sheep; but all they see is an amazing lion!

Similar to what drives perfectionism in some individuals, imposter syndrome is often (but not exclusively) the result of three types of circumstances. The first is growing up in a family system that either dismissed or minimized your accomplishments or treated them as minimum standards to be met. While some recognition may have been displayed, there was not enough to help your little girl brain internalize your accomplishments as really, really great ones!

Secondly, high perfectionism results from you holding yourself hostage to every mistake you've made and then using those mistakes as justification for why you really don't have a right to be viewed in such a positive light.

Lastly, imposter syndrome can also manifest from being a survivor of abuse (i.e, physical, emotional, or otherwise). Allow me to explain this one a bit further. I've worked with survivors of childhood abuse who have grown to become successful and accomplished women who struggled with imposter syndrome. But for those who did not have an opportunity early on to effectively process their abuse and its impact on their sense of self, they came to assume and cultivate the belief that they were in some way "bad." Bad for allowing the abuse to happen or bad as a result of it happening. This inaccurate perception of self laid the foundation for some really harsh self-talk and generated an unhealthy way of coping. Mistakes throughout life only reinforced the negative self-talk. Nonetheless, with each achieved success in their careers, that voice never really disappeared; it just morphed into something uglier. So, when these women actually created successful lives for themselves, the sense of "if they only knew how bad I am" camouflaged itself into statements like:

- I am a fraud.

- I do not deserve success or professional accolades for doing what I am supposed to do.

- People believe that I am more competent than I really am.

- I've just gotten lucky. I can't do this again.

- There are other people who deserve to be here with way more experience.

Now I want to admit that I just got super "therapisty"—please forgive me. However, I do want to be clear that I am not saying that all survivors of abuse will struggle with imposter syndrome. Rather, I am simply providing an example to highlight the fact that in the extreme, imposter syndrome can have some rather complex roots and/or origin stories.

So How Can You Combat Fear and Scarcity in Your Daily Life?

As Always, Get Oriented

Here's what I know to be true: Fear is a natural part of growth. However, when your fears go unchecked, they can morph into behaviors that drive incongruence and end up running (and sometimes ruining) your business, your relationships, and your life. Yet, here's the good news: Once you understand your fears and how they manifest, you can better navigate and challenge them in your day to day.

There are two activities that I like to assign to help you better understand and challenge your fears. The first, you can consider a more comprehensive reflection and the second is more specific to facing your fears as it relates to specific goals; both can be found and completed in the digital companion journal.

To facilitate this reflection, I like to assign the following activity:

Grab a sheet out of your journal and fold it into three parts. Label the first column **"What I am afraid of."** This is a no judgment zone, so allow yourself to be honest and even irrational here! Don't just limit yourself to your professional aspirations—consider relational fears too! It's just you and this sheet of paper, so get to listing. Label the second column, **"How do I try to prevent this fear from happening?"** When answering this question, really think about the things you DO to avoid and or protect yourself from the manifestation of this fear. At the top of the third column, write, **"Is the way that I am responding to this fear moving me towards my valued direction or keeping me stuck? How?"** Be really honest here. Now if you didn't use the earlier reflection activity to define your valued direction, I am going to ask that you stop and go back to that activity. None of this work will feel like it's worth doing if you don't have an identified valued direction worth doing it for. Once it's complete, it will look a little something like the chart below. Remember you are creating a list and challenging it.

What am I afraid of?	How do I prevent it?	Does this fear or the actions I am taking to prevent this fear move me closer or keep me stuck? How?
Ex: Not living up to my potential; being irrelevant.	*I try to do everything perfectly. Don't take risks. Afraid to make mistakes. Often take on more than I should.*	*No. Keeps me stuck. I want to start my own business, but I am afraid of failing at it, then what?*

Once you have identified the fears that are keeping you stuck, highlight them. On a separate sheet of paper in your journal, consider the ways that you can shift how you're responding to these fears using the following question prompts:

- When did this fear enter my life?

    Ex: Definitely middle school

- Did I inherit this fear? Or was this fear the product of my own experience?

    Ex: A little of both…

- What would a more values-oriented response to this fear look like?

    Ex: Although not living up to my potential is scary, trying to be perfect exhausts me and goes against my values of grace, knowledge, and self-acceptance. I can work on setting more realistic expectations for myself and not allowing myself to wrap so much of my success up in being perfect.

- Will I need help to put this revised perspective into practice?

    Ex: Yes, I don't know where to begin.

I also absolutely love Russ Harris's F.E.A.R. vs. D.A.R.E. activity. It is a great way to determine specifically how fear is impacting your ability to follow through on your big beautiful goals. Rather than trying to explain it here, you can access it in the companion journal.

Watch What You Say and How You Say It

It is very important that you embrace the idea that as a true practitioner of your health and wellness, you must also become intentional and deliberate with your words, thoughts, and actions. Not to the point of scrutiny, of course, but to the point of being present in how these states impact your energetic frequencies and thus output. This will naturally require you to slow down and listen to yourself. The language that we use to describe our circumstances sometimes inadvertently reinforces a lack of agency and scarcity mindset. For example, I often interacted with money from a complete place of scarcity. I used to say things like "investing intimidates me" or I would use the word "broke" to define my low funds (e.g., "I am broke," "I am tapped out," etc.). In these examples, I was not only using my language to define my circumstances from a place of scarcity, but this same language was also defining me how I operated on a sub-conscious level! This brings me to my next point: thinking in abundance.

Abundance is really your ability to see more in your life: more options, more choices, more resources, more freedom, etc. When we are operating in our fear-based mindset (whether consciously or subconsciously), we're unable to really see the bigger picture. This is pretty normal. But when we allow ourselves to shift to an abundance mindset, we allow ourselves to operate in the knowledge that even when we ourselves feel limited, there are resources available to us. We just have to allow ourselves to do the work that removes the beliefs and rules blocking our clarity. Now I know I have made this shift sound super easy. Like everything I have shared up to this point, thoughtful intention and consistent practice is the secret sauce. Truthfully, where folks often struggle is the believability of their abundance thinking. In other words, my clients often ask, "do I have to believe what I am saying?" My reply, "It certainly helps!" It also helps if you are operating in reality. Sometimes speaking and thinking in abundance is confused with wishful thinking. For example:

- **Scarcity statement:** I don't want to depend on anyone. So, I'll start my business when I have earned all the seed money.

- **Abundance statement:** I can start building the foundation of my business today. I can create the wealth I need to build a thriving business over time.

- **Wishful thinking:** My business is a good one. I am pretty sure I can secure the money I need with some good marketing.

The point I am making here is that what you say and how you say it is that much more dynamic when paired with an abundance mindset. Check out the companion journal to get some practice!

Recalibrate Your Personal Agency and Shift Your Focus

If you are unfamiliar with personal agency (also known as one's locus of control), it is an all-encompassing term that describes the degree of power that an individual believes they have over their own life. More specifically, it is a subjective measure that determines the degree to which you feel that you have control over your mind, body, and environment.

To help grasp this concept, Franklin Covey created an interesting distinction between our "Circle of Concern" and our "Circle of Control." Circles of Concern are the things that you often waste time and energy worrying about, but that you have little to no control over. In our circles of concern, we are not operating optimally in our personal agency. Meanwhile, Circles of Control are the things that you can influence in your daily life, resulting in an increase in personal agency.

As an example, the vast majority of news stories—about everything from political scandal and terrorism to the economy, celebrity gossip, and who your ex is dating—fall squarely within the Circle of Concern. They can easily soak up your time and energy, but you have virtually no control over these things.

Other examples include getting angry about what someone posted on Instagram, worrying about what other people think about you, or wishing your loved ones would make better choices (a valid wish, but still outside of your control). For all of you visual learners I have included an example in the figure below.

Circle of Concern vs. Circle of Control

(-) Personal Agency

A large circle of concern and small circle of control means more emphasis is placed on past mistakes, what others are doing & thinking, etc. You are thus living life reactively.

(+) Personal Agency

When operating within a small circle of concern and a large circle of control. More emphasis is placed on what is within your control. You are thus living life proactively.

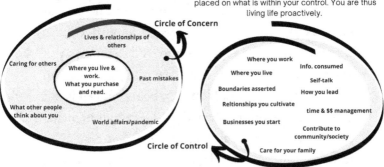

Since ego-driven fear is often the result of perceived threats from factors out of our control, using this tool to facilitate insight can be a valuable tool. Not only does making the shift from operating in your Circle of Concern to your Circle of Control increase your personal agency. It allows you to live life less reactively and more proactive. If you are someone who struggles with anxiety this is a great way to hone in on what is contributing to your worries. Even on its surface, awareness of this distinction can help you see the personal agency that you already have.

Define What Failure and Success Actually Mean to You

I remember speaking to one of my mentees and during our conversation, we came around to the topic of her potentially failing in her business. She flat out said, "Nikki, I know in business we have to learn to accept failure, but I don't want to!" I'll share with you what I shared with her: You're definitely going to fail in life and in business. However, being aligned is not about being comfortable with it—it's about knowing exactly what failure and success mean to you. Not to your momma, your daddy, or the world, but you! And when you define failure for yourself, also define what it means to be successful. Then, when you've defined both, check them against your values and your valued direction. Do these definitions motivate you to move in your valued direction or will they get you caught up in fear?

Challenge Your Inner Critic and Dispute Negative Thoughts

Don't let your inner critic be the cause of your demise. Turn down the volume on that negativity by amplifying your connection to your highest self. When my inner critic is trying to take me out, I refer directly to my values. I ask myself, "Is there a kinder way that I can talk to myself in this moment?" You'd be surprised how small things practiced consistently can drive big change. If this is an area where you struggle, this is exactly what make therapy and even life coaching so helpful!

Practice Saying No

As high achievers, our ambition drives us to test our capacity and take on as much as we can mentally bear. However, setting healthy boundaries is the very thing that leads to sustainable energy in this marathon called life. In becoming a more congruent woman, one of your responsibilities will be to learn how to discern between a good thing and a G-d thing—and please note that not all good things are actually G-d things. A good thing or opportunity is anything that comes from your hard work or simply being a good person. A G-d thing is a Divine order that aligns with your purpose and thus your heart's deepest desire. I realized within my own process that because I was filling my figurative plate with all of the good things, I never really had room to enjoy the things that G-d was calling me to tackle. This posed a real problem on my path towards my valued direction. While I was saying yes to the things that I thought I was supposed to be doing, I was saying no to the things that I was being called to do. Four questions that you'll want to get comfortable asking are:

- Will this move me towards my valued direction or keep me stuck?

- If I say no to this, what am I saying yes to?

- If I say yes to this what am I saying no to?

- Can I mentally and emotionally afford to add this to my plate?

Recognize the Difference Between Healthy Striving and Perfectionism

Brené Brown—an American scholar, author, and public speaker—describes healthy striving as seeking excellence from a place of wholeness, a place where you're happy with who you are and you know that you can be even better. Perfectionism, on the other hand, comes from a feeling of not being good enough. People who are perfectionists think that if they achieve X or Y standard, they'll finally be able to feel good about themselves. To put it another way, healthy striving is about honoring yourself by endeavoring to achieve your full potential.

Perfectionism is about dishonoring yourself by telling yourself that there are certain things that you need to achieve before you're "enough."

Set Realistic Goals

Perfectionism is only a problem because we have underbudgeted for difficulty, not because we are aiming high. It strikes when we imagine that we might write a good novel in six months or have a good career by the age of 30 or have spontaneously worked out how to have a successful marriage. Setting goals that are completely out of our reach is a great way to promote incongruence and the negative self-talk that comes with being out of alignment with your values and valued direction. The solution then is to start setting realistic goals that require you to stretch some, but also increase the likelihood of success. Once you reach your realistic goal, set another goal that's just a little further off. Keep going in this way and you'll soon realize that you've made a lot of progress.

Reflection Questions:

- What does failure really mean to you? What would it look like if you were actually failing in life, in your career or relationships?

- What does success really mean to you? What would it look like if you were succeeding in life, in your career or relationships? Now take a look at your responses. Are there any unrealistic expectations hiding out?

- If you could write a want ad seeking a more confident and aligned voice, what qualities and characteristics would you look for?

If you haven't had a chance to check out the companion journal, please do so now! I have included a number of exercises and reflection prompts to help you confront fear and scarcity in a more thoughtful manner.

DEFINING EXCEPTIONAL

*My mission in life is not merely to survive, but
to thrive; and to do so with some passion, some
compassion, some humor, and some style.*
—*Maya Angelou*

She is known to many as the Strong Black Woman or
Black Superwoman. Although well intentioned, we
know that her standards are difficult to sustain and
often result in exhaustion. Still, her code of conduct
is woven into our genetic makeup and, seemingly
unwittingly, we find ourselves in pursuit of her image.
What does this look like? Generally, it manifests as an
inherent sense of duty to take on the world and all
of its problems, while juggling our Blackness and our
womanhood. This deeply rooted obligation to do it
all and be it all is not new, even though our rational

selves know that achieving "all" is a nearly impossible feat.

While it is evident that our ancestral mothers had to cultivate personas of strength to reject negative societal characterizations of their womanhood, we must also remember that this image of "good Black womanhood" served as a mechanism of survival and leadership in the face of horrendous trauma. As opposed to the cult of true womanhood, an early 19th century ideal, primarily embraced by white Christian Americans who believed that good women were supposed to possess four cardinal virtues: piety, purity, domesticity, and submissiveness. Our value (even in the eyes of our men) was measured by our ability to endure, rise above, and serve in a sociopolitical climate that openly endorsed violent racism, gender-based oppression, health inequity, disenfranchisement, and limited resources, thus birthing an image and an unwritten code of conduct passed down through generations of women who are amply equipped with instructions on how to problem solve and show up and show out in the world. The Strong Black Woman's code of conduct declares that good, strong, Black women should:

- Present an image of strength at all times and resist the expression of vulnerability, unless in grief. "Don't let anyone see you cry—they'll just use it against you."

- "Push through" emotional and psychological discomfort. "Suck it up."

- Maintain a persistent heir of humility and gratitude. "Be humble."

- Operate in forgiveness as good, G-d-fearing women are instructed.

- Attend church regularly. "You better have Psalms 23 remembered."

- Work hard without complaint. "Be grateful that you have a job."

- Don't be a burden. "Ain't nobody got time for that."

Now to be clear, these are just some of the nuts and bolts. Every woman has a vision shaped by the women that came before her. When I speak to my now 90-year-old grandmother, who raised six young Black men on her own, I get the sense that one of the challenges she faced in adhering to this code was navigating the very complicated path between being both strong and subservient. I imagine that this was the case for many Black women who were in many instances the primary breadwinners, but not necessarily accepted by mainstream standards as the heads of their households.

Yet a shift occurred as more Black women wrestled with this dichotomy and set their sights on the horizon of possibility. The Strong Black Woman's code of conduct expanded to better encompass our ambition, giving life to the idea that we must be both strong and exceptional! In this revision, the focus was still on our fortitude, survival, and advancement. However, for those more progressive-thinking sistahs, this shift coupled with determination catapulted their entry into the fields of medicine, law, government, science, engineering, and beyond, prompting greater emphasis on our ability to drive change, succeed at all costs, and to do so with both poise and perfection. In the words of Nannie Helen Burroughs, a Black educator, orator, religious leader, civil rights activist, feminist, and businesswoman of the early 20th century, "To struggle and battle and overcome and absolutely defeat every force designed against us is the only way to achieve." Or even as

Sheila Radford-Hill (2002, io86) describes, a strong Black woman typically learns from women kin to combine "attitude, altitude, image, and faith" so as to develop "a self-concept that [can] withstand the all-too-common experiences of male rejection, economic deprivation, crushing family responsibilities, and countless forms of discrimination." Woosah, as I can go on. I could write a whole book exploring the complex psychological impact of the superwoman persona on the Black female experience, but that is not the goal here. Instead, it is to bring a point of concern into awareness.

While many of us have our own ideas about what it means to be a Strong Black Woman, we also recognize that her code of conduct is both a blessing and a system of rules in desperate need of revision. While this code has helped frame our experiences and aid in our ability to successfully navigate difficult landscapes both personally and professionally, it also perpetuates fear and isolation. It fosters a fragmented connection to self that seeds the kind of beliefs that today pose as real barriers to our congruence and alignment to our higher selves, as well as the dreams and legacies that we wish to manifest. It is only natural, then, that we actively seek to revise this image. However, whether it is donning the T-shirt of a magical Black Girl or the coat of an exceptional Black woman as we pursue our own congruence, it is important to ensure that these labels are not simply new ways to promote the same benevolent fictional character with superhuman powers.

In other words, even in our desire to be exceptional, we must ask ourselves, "Am I still unconsciously operating under the oppressive narrative that as a Black woman, I must be extraordinary in order for my life and place on this earth to be deemed valuable and secure? If you're uncertain, consider the following: Have you become a manic overachiever in your life? Or does the idea of your so-called mediocrity fill you with shame and an intense urgency to accomplish?

Please forgive me if the tone feels harsh, as adding gas to that fire certainly isn't my intent. However, what I have come to learn over the years through observation and direct conversations with other women is that while Black women— especially Black professional women—do struggle with perfectionism and imposter syndrome, these challenges may have more to do with the fact that we are inherently struggling with what it means to clearly define our exceptionalism without sounding like Superwoman! If we are not making a significant impact or quantifiable influence across a sliding scale in some capacity, then we feel like we're falling short. If our shit is not all the way together, we are falling short. If we don't have the followers, we're falling short. If we give a kick-ass presentation, but miss a few points that we really wanted to make but were not super critical, we're falling short!

Let's take a beat and consider what would happen if we allowed and empowered ourselves to define what it means to be exceptional within the context of our own defined values and valued directions. What if we accepted and operated as exceptional beings seeking excellence from a place of wholeness instead of deficiency? What if we simply pursued harmony?

Harmony

Harmony makes small things grow, lack of it makes great things decay.
—Sallust

Some time ago and while running one of my many Sunday errands, I remember listening to my daughter going on and on about everything she plans to accomplish in her life. In her own words, she wants to get drafted into the WNBA, launch a makeup empire, and become a music engineer. Oh, and how can I forget, she also wants to dance professionally. I smile, not because her plan has a whole lot of working parts to it, but because in her heart of hearts, these are all attainable goals; and who am I to adult all over her 10-year-old dreams? However, I did think for a moment about who I was as a 10-year-old girl. When did I learn to dream within the lines? When did my vision become so damn practical?! When did it become a rule of thumb to balance what I loved doing with what I needed or was expected to do?

I'll go as far as to assume that you have also, at some point in your life, asked yourself some variation of these questions, and since you're reading this book, you're probably asking them now.

One of the ideas that I have come to dread is that of balance, especially the terms "work-life balance" or "home-life balance." A little piece of me cries when I hear these words. As a mother of two, wife to an entrepreneur, business owner, daughter, friend, mentor, professor, etcetera, etcetera, the idea of balance just seems to be a nonsensical one. Like many of you, I'll admit that there was a time when I was determined to plant my flag and declare that I had achieved the ever-moving target of balance. To do so would mean that I had finally figured it all out! Well, I am pretty damn set on the fact that on a macro level, balance just doesn't exist. So, I have embraced wholeheartedly the realism in striving to achieve harmony in my life. This aspiration has lent itself to my exceptionalism.

Unlike the idea of balance, which promotes the idea of equilibrium or equal distribution of weight, responsibility, etc., to live in harmony is to do the things we love with whom we love doing them. To live in harmony necessitates that we as Black women accept our innate right to define ourselves, our right to live consistently with our most profound feelings of what is genuine and what matters most. Living in harmony necessitates that we be aware of the expectations and requirements that encompass us, and that we adapt in our own way. To seek harmony means to journey inwards and outwards. It is to understand that we can only live in concordance with others when we are in agreement with our Divine selves. It is understanding that the outward journey is an extension of an inner one, which allows us to live well within ourselves and to achieve fulfillment in the mental, physical, and spiritual aspects of our lives. To live harmoniously is to fully embrace the idea that the Universe flows through our veins and with every beat of our hearts. To live in harmony is to exist in unison with this understanding. Now, what would the partners you choose, the issues that you tolerate, the conversations that you entertain, the opportunities that you seek, and the goals that you set for yourself look like if you operated in this congruence? Imagine the source of love that you could tap into. Imagine what it would feel like to create from this harmonious space.

Whether we can connect to it or not, human beings instinctively seek harmony—harmony in our relationships with others, harmony with our environments, and above all, harmony within ourselves. Every day we witness the rising and setting of the sun, the regal calm of the moon. We have all structured our lives according to the cycle of the four seasons. This is proof that harmony not only exists, but is also realistic and attainable.

This shift in my own processing has been a game changer. In harmony, I am less judgmental of myself. In harmony, there is an acceptance that sometimes I can't do it all. Because the reality is, more often than not, I cannot ensure the equal distribution of resources, also known as my time. In harmony, I get to love and interact with others transparently. My kids know when mommy is tired and needs rest and this truth does not become their burden. They know when a busy and demanding week may make me less visible around the house. But they also see and feel my effort of love in the moments that we do cherish together. Even my marriage has improved. I am no longer stressing out over my inability to achieve the false milestones that society sets for a good wife. I am sorry, but if I just worked a 60-hour week, managed to cook a real dinner four nights out of said workweek, and mother my kids for my husband, we are not having hot, passionate sex every single night just because some damn man has convinced women that it's the best way to keep their husbands. Gurl, bye!! If that is your schtick, boo, have at it. But my definition of harmony allows me to honor my own needs in the midst of taking everyone else's into account without guilt. Cultivating harmony in my life has also been restorative. I have found more energy to do the things I love and that has been transformative in and of itself. There was a time in my life when I only had time to grind; but now, I play and dance with my kids. I take long walks with my husband. I hang out with friends and I set healthy boundaries around how much time I give to my business. This, my friend, has allowed me to feel exceptional!

Reflection Questions:

- Take a moment to reflect on what harmony means to you.

- Where in your life do you feel the most harmonious and/or disharmonious? Why?

- What could harmony look like in actual practice?

HEALING OUR INNER CHILD

Our fear of healing our wounds properly is also the fear that preserves them.
—*Nichomi Higgins*

In the words of Maya Angelou,

> The Black female is assaulted in her tender years by all those common forces of nature at the same time that she is caught in the tripartite crossfire of masculine prejudice, white illogical hate, and Black lack of power.

> The fact that the adult American Negro female emerges a formidable character is often met with amazement, distaste, and

even belligerence. It is seldom accepted as an inevitable outcome of the struggle won by survivors and deserves respect if not enthusiastic acceptance.

Like most of you, I have always been aware of the simple truth that despite its beauty, life can also be hard and unjust. This somber awareness has never really brought me any comfort; I don't imagine that it's supposed to. It doesn't temper the range of emotions that I experience when I am first allowed into the dark, fragile, and scary spaces of a person's painful memories. It has yet to reduce the angst that comes with my ability to absorb the world's joys and stresses like a big ole "emotional sponge," nor has it nullified the ugly truth that far too many Black women have silently incurred the wounds of emotional and physical mishandling at the hands of people who were supposed to protect and care for them.

What does ground me is the understanding that we, as Black women, have a unique ability to love, transform, create, rise above, and become greater than our pain, despite our hardships. But this requires us to summon the courage to attend to our wounds like a loving mother to her child. Although this may sound simple, for so many the word mother may invoke a convoluted web of opposing feelings.

In this perspective, I'd like to introduce the concept of the inner child. Specifically, the significant healing that can occur when we create space within our lives to acknowledge compassionately that this aspect of ourselves exists. To some, the idea of reconnecting to one's inner child may sound foreign and odd. I think that's fair. For many Black women, the ability to embrace our inner child is problematic because, as little Black girls, many of us were not able to exist in a childlike state. As a result, the idea of connecting to our innocence and vulnerability can feel scary and, for some, unsafe. However, for true metamorphosis and alignment to occur, we must be willing to heal at all levels of ourselves. Remember what I said—although the phase of ego confrontation will take time, beauty does and will emerge in the process.

With that said, I want to emphasize that the inner child is real. Not literally, nor physically, but figuratively real. It is a psychological reality that is a crucial aspect of the woman you are today and the congruent woman that you are becoming. While the depth and breadth of inner child work can look different for everyone, its relevance to the work completed in the phase of ego confrontation is crucial. Many of the behavioral, emotional, and relationship difficulties that we experience in adulthood today stem from childhood interpretations.

In my professional opinion, acknowledging and processing how one's inner child shows up in the world today is a compelling aspect of the therapeutic process. This is the aspect of ourselves that holds the accumulated hurts, traumas, fears, and angers of our youth. It is essential to note that the inner child is composed of the self from birth to about 19 years of age. Within these years of critical development, we are supposed to learn how to relate to others, communicate and assert ourselves. We also learn how to cope in healthy and unhealthy ways. It was during these stages of development that you absorbed your parents' patterns of behavior and communication, and when you formed your initial value system. Those lessons and experiences—good, bad, or otherwise— became the foundation of your adult perspectives. For example, many of the negative messages that you tell yourself and negative feelings that you hold about your body today as an adult originated in the period of your life between the ages of three and six years old. During this stage of life, the foundation for your self-worth was being laid. If you were taught that you were basically good, but that sometimes you did bad things, you probably would have developed a solid foundation on which to build your self-worth.

On the other hand, if you were reprimanded continuously as a child, you would grow up adopting and applying that language to yourself any time you made a mistake. This is also an applicable explanation for those of you who grew up without one or both of your biological parents. While you may not have been told that you were terrible, the mere absence of your parents seeded this belief. Please note that the example I have shared here is pretty straightforward.

While I am confident that many of us can speak to positive experiences in our earlier days, I am sure that we can also speak to notably difficult ones. As we age, connect, accomplish, and abide by our code of conduct, it is normal to become convinced that we have successfully outgrown this child and their emotional baggage; but this can be far from the truth for a lot of us. In fact, for many, the intense desire to escape or quickly move on from their past has resulted in various avoidant coping strategies that have ultimately become problematic barriers to the lives and relationships they desire to experience. In the words of Dr. Stephen A. Diamond:

True adulthood hinges on acknowledging, accepting, and taking responsibility for loving and parenting one's own inner child. For most adults, this never happens. Instead, their inner child has been denied, neglected, disparaged, abandoned, or rejected. We are told by society to "grow up," putting childish things aside. To become adults, we've been taught that our inner child—representing our childlike capacity for innocence, wonder, awe, joy, sensitivity, and playfulness—must be stifled, quarantined, or even killed.

Unwittingly, we are constantly being influenced or covertly controlled by this unconscious version of ourselves. For many, it is not an adult that is self-directing their lives, but rather an emotionally wounded inner child inhabiting an adult body. Or as I like to say, a five-year-old running around in a forty-year-old frame. It is a hurt, angry, fearful little kid or teen calling the shots. A five- or ten-year-old (or both of them!) trying to engage in grown-up relationships. And then we wonder why our relationships fall apart. Why do we feel so anxious? Afraid? Insecure? Inferior? Small? Lost? Lonely? But think about it: How else would a child feel having to fend for themselves in an adult world without proper parental supervision, protection, structure, or support?

Let's take a moment to examine these connections at a broader level. Generally speaking, if your parents or guardians didn't often or regularly show interest in your emotional needs for love, support, protection, and/or guidance; if you grew up feeling unheard, invalidated, or unseen, or were otherwise condemned for your emotional expression, you may:

- Experience high self-criticism and low self-worth

- Often ignore or avoid your own emotional needs, resulting in somatic illness

- Have developed deep-seated anger issues

- Have developed unhealthy or unproductive ways of coping in order to have a sense of comfort and safety within your life

- Have developed psychological and/or physical illnesses

- Have problems sustaining healthy and/or committed and respectful relationships

If, on a fundamental level, you grew up feeling unsafe due to a traumatic experience or abuse (of any kind), the following issues can develop:

- Low self-worth resulting in physical neglect/ abuse of oneself (e.g., eating disorders, maintaining an unhealthy diet, self-harm)

- Intense safety-seeking behaviors or extreme risk-taking behaviors (e.g., unprotected sex, obsessive daredevil feats, etc.)

- Addictions to drugs, alcohol, violence, food, etc.

- Amplified experience of shame, guilt, and expressions of anger

Or maybe you have not experienced the above explicitly, but you can relate to the following:

- I am afraid to take risks.

- I'm a people pleaser and tend to lack a strong identity.

- I tend to hoard things and have trouble letting go.

- I always criticize myself for being inadequate, even though I rationally know that I am not.

- I have trouble starting or finishing major projects.

- I have sex when I don't really want to.

- I avoid conflict at all costs.

- I feel more responsible for others than for myself.

- My deepest fear is being abandoned or rejected, and I'll do anything to hold onto a relationship.

When our inner child is blocked, we are robbed of our natural spontaneity and zest for life. When our inner child is hidden, so are we. These are just some of the examples that indicate that your wounded inner child is operating in your life. At this point, you may be asking yourself, "What does the work look like?" I want to start by clearly stating that if your younger days include traumatic experiences, i.e., abuse, neglect, significant loss, exposure to violence, etc., I will encourage you to unpack this work with a professional, specifically one who specializes in trauma. Although there are some good workbooks out there, please do not try to take this work on by yourself. Trained clinicians have the skillsets and tools to develop a comprehensive treatment plan with your safety and well-being in mind.

I personally gravitate towards the power therapies when working with my clients. These include eye movement desensitization and reprocessing (EMDR) and Brainspotting. Both are extremely powerful and effective trauma-focused modalities. Since everyone's experiences are unique and not everyone has to do a deep dive into their childhood to connect to this past source of their current pain, some of you may be able to facilitate this work on your own. Suppose you do not have a significant history of trauma and would like to begin the process of self-exploration. In that case, the primary goals of this work are threefold.

First, one has to become conscious of their inner child. Remaining unconscious is what empowers this version of self to hop into the driver's seat of your life. This process entails naming the pain from your earlier years and the coinciding emotions and beliefs that accompanied them. For example, through my work, I learned that my childhood self from ages 10 to 14 was a significant source of my earlier pain and meaning making. While I do not have a history of trauma, I experienced other events that greatly influenced my identity and sense of belonging.

Second, because the pain that we are holding and how we are holding it isn't always evident, you must be willing to examine how your coping strategies are attached to it. Trauma, disappointment, and loss that go unnamed become stored unknowns—harbored in the heart, the mind, and the body. The symptoms that emerge from these accumulated experiences may worsen or manifest in the form of disordered eating (e.g., binge eating, not eating, purging, etc.), disconnection from the body resulting in poor self-image or impaired physical intimacy, frequent dissociation when overwhelmed, recurring physical pain (e.g., regular neck and backaches, headaches, pain in our reproductive systems, etc.). These symptoms might also coincide with depression, anxiety, PTSD, substance abuse, impulsivity, and more.

Third, you must be open and willing to self-parent yourself through the process of revising your faulty narratives. As a quick refresher, I use the term "faulty meaning" to encapsulate any beliefs, rules, or assumptions that collude with your ego-driven fear and impair your ability to move toward your valued direction. This is a critical part of the work because the whole purpose is to recalibrate rules and beliefs associated with experiences that some of us would rather not address. Through self-parenting, we can also learn to practice the language of grace and compassion towards ourselves. Again, under the guidance of a trained and licensed therapist who has experience facilitating this trauma-centered work, real progress can be made!

Take a few moments to breathe and connect with yourself. Remember what I said. Change and growth is an anointed process. While awareness can be uncomfortable, it can also liberate. However, like most of the change process, connecting to your inner child is an ongoing process, and you, my friend, are not alone. So, I encourage you to take your time and go slowly; being gentle with yourself is vital.

All of us have experiences that have shaped how we make sense of ourselves today, and if you have not, that's okay too. But for those of you that can relate, it's helpful to remember that while some, or even many, of our problems stem from childhood, people are often the victims of victims. Becoming an adult means swallowing this "bitter pill" and taking on the responsibility for taking care of that inner child's needs today.

To get this point across, I'd like to share the following metaphor:

Imagine yourself driving down the road of life towards your valued direction, but you're not in the driver's seat. Instead, it's your 5, 10, 12, or 13-year-old self behind the wheel. You're buckled into the passenger's seat, and your highest self is patiently sitting in the back seat. Now that you're aware of who may be driving your vehicle, you have a choice to make. You can choose to remain in the passenger seat because, truth be told, that little version of yourself has gotten you pretty far in life. Or you can get into the driver's seat, move your highest self into the passenger seat, and move that little self to the back seat. Now, your little self is not just going to move to the back seat; her feelings will be hurt, and she will be afraid that you are moving her there because she's done something wrong. She will throw a tantrum; her fear will peak, and she'll really tell you how horrible you are. So, what are you to do?! Well, connecting to your inner child is instructing that version of yourself to pull over to the side of the road. Once pulled over, you will need to talk to her lovingly. You will need to thank her for her determination and resilience. Acknowledge her hurt and pain, because invalidation will only perpetuate the problem. Then you will need to explain to her why it is time for you and your highest self to move into position in the front, and why you need her help from the back seat. We don't want her out of the car; she is more than her struggles and she has so much to offer. But her job as the driver is finally done. Once you have done that, you begin to get her to trust you.

The point that I am trying to make is that, as with much of therapy, the process of learning to connect with and nurture your inner child is a learning process. If we can recognize this problem for what it is, we can begin a different, deeper, more meaningful type of healing. I want to validate that this work will come with resistance, specifically in the form of fear—fear of opening old wounds, fear of being taken advantage of, etc. But this fear should not be a hindrance to the anointed growth we desire because as we learn to connect to this version of ourselves, we do so precisely as a good parent relates to a flesh-and-blood child: providing nurture, acceptance, boundaries, and structure. These are indispensable elements of loving and living with any child, whether metaphorical or actual. By initiating and maintaining an ongoing dialogue between the two, a reconciliation between inner child and mature adult can be reached. A new, mutually beneficial relationship can be created in which the sometimes-conflicting needs of both can be creatively satisfied.

So if you take nothing else away from this perspective, I hope that you can allow yourself to embrace the idea that within our Western way of life, human beings are starving for relief from the burden of their pain and convinced that to truly heal, they have to repair the cracks and restore themselves back to a form that never appeared broken at all. Some are told that true healing happens when the broken pieces are discarded altogether. The pressure to heal in such a way creates additional anxiety and further perpetuates perfectionism and the belief that we are not good enough, so we find ourselves stuck and hungry for answers. We turn to a system designed to profit from both our perceived inadequacies and our desire to BE and FEEL good...enough. We try to discard our "bad" pieces and conceal our cracks in meaningful and meaningless ways, hoping that peace will come or questioning the meaning of life when it does not, all the while fearing this simple truth: Healing happens when you stop trying to disown the bad and instead allow yourself to examine your fragments—your parts, your broken pieces—and assign them NEW meaning. Meaning that promotes your value and honors your integrity as an imperfect human vessel. Once you have accepted your G-d-given ability to CREATE meaning and shift your perspective (I know it's hard), you can then experience the freedom of self-acceptance, cracks and all—the finished product something like *kintsugi*.

If you are unfamiliar with the term *kintsugi*, it is a Japanese art or method of pottery repair that highlights the artifact's unique history and beauty by emphasizing the cracks using gold, platinum, or silver lacquer. *Kintsugi*, I believe, is a beautiful example that highlights the beauty of who we are, flaws and all.

Reflection Questions:

Take a look at the companion journal to view a few of the inner child activities that I have cooked up.

ESTABLISHING CERTAINTY IN UNCERTAINTY

On a fundamental level, we must operate in the understanding that every single day is a blessing filled with uncertainty. Still, we push through, we set plans, we connect dots, and we exist. But I often wonder, when do we become overpowered by the uncertainty of life and why? Uncertainty is not a new phenomenon and yet, when faced with it, we momentarily lose all sense of our strengths, resources, and assets. One of the tools that I often use to navigate uncertainty is actually a series of questions: **What? How? What? How?**

At first glance, the only question that comes to mind may be, "What the hell is that?" Or maybe I am being dramatic with my assumptions. Either way, these two simple questions, repeated in sequence, are a true game changer. They can be used to navigate just about any perceived obstacle or period of uncertainty that you might face (or are currently facing) in your life. And this little formula will also serve as the framework for helping you embrace your highest self and thrive accordingly! Because my mantra has always been, keep the process simple and consistent enough so that people can actually follow it, I am always looking for ways to help my clients take what they learn in session out into the world. I came up with this little formula four years ago in a couple's session. I was teaching the couple how to come together after arguments and effectively navigate repairing conversations. As the instructions were coming out of my mouth, I remember thinking, "This is so damn practical! Why not try to use it for everything?!" So, I did, and over the years it has helped countless people move through their ish—especially in times of uncertainty. Hell, I employ it every day!

Here's How It Works

Your What

The first "What?" is all about getting clear on what it is that you want to achieve or accomplish. Whether you're asking yourself "What do I want to accomplish today?"; "What do I want to accomplish in my life?"; or "What do I want to accomplish in this conversation?" this question gets us thinking more clearly about the desired outcome. Naturally, this results in a greater feeling of orientation. Other ways that I ask this question are "What is your valued direction?" or "What is the vision that you are trying to bring to life?" We will dive deeper soon.

Your How

Now, the next question is also pretty straightforward. When I ask my clients to consider their "how?" I am basically asking them to consider how they want to go about achieving their desired outcome. To be fair, this question is really easy when it comes to day-to-day responsibilities, but when we start talking about visions, passions, and careers, then sometimes I get "I don't know!" Other times, clients may share a few ideas. However, more often than not, I get a roadmap with a simple "x" to denote the destination.

The Next What

The second half of this formula is where it gets introspective, because this question requires you to get honest about your ways of thinking and doing that might impair your ability to achieve your desired outcome. As you can imagine, it's pretty easy to find the culprits outside of you. That is why I encourage my clients to ask, "What might I be doing to hinder my steps?" This shift in responsibility is a true game changer.

The How (aka the Getting Unstuck)

Finally, the last how is where introspection meets action, my friends! Here, I am asking you to ask yourself, "How am I going to overcome the barriers that I have identified?"—especially when those barriers include you! I admit that this question is a bit daunting and can be disheartening, but it's important to acknowledge that successfully moving through this part of the formula will take a bit of grace, effort, time, and support! It can only be done when you are truly ready to confront, embrace, and work through all of the impediments that are blocking your progression along life's journey.

Now, if you're one of those ladies that likes to ask why, you may be wondering why you're not seeing it in this little formula. Questions like, "Why am I here?" "Why do I keep making the same choices?" are all good questions that in many cases you've been asking yourself for some time now. However, insight without action is simply insight. I have watched clients find painful and sometimes more confusing answers to their why questions, only to continue struggling with the problem. Sometimes asking why can give the illusion of progress when in reality, we are only digging ourselves deeper into the problem. To clarify, I am not saying that you should kill self-exploration. I am just saying that once your answers start to repeat themselves, the real work comes when you ask, "What's next?"

Now there is a caveat. When I do encourage my clients to reflect upon their why, it has less to do with cause and everything to do with intention. In other words, "Why do you want the thing that you want?" We'll explore further in a bit.

I have inserted this perspective for two reasons:

First, we all know that life is not going to stop in order for you to achieve a peaceful process of change. Balancing growth with life's day-to-day responsibilities can often leave you feeling overwhelmed. Even if clarity is all around you, accessing it may be difficult, especially when you're in the thick of confronting yourself.

Second, as you begin to clear the mental and emotional roadblocks that cast a shadow on your clarity and impair your congruence, you will naturally get more clarity! Puzzle pieces will begin to fit together, and the destination will become more obvious. In these moments, you can feel so inspired and driven to create that having a tool to help you organize your thoughts can be very helpful.

In sum, What, How, What, How is all about asking what do you want to achieve, how do you want to get there, what might get in your way, and how do you best push past roadblocks to overcome it?

Reflection Questions:

Let's try it out! Think of a small or large goal that you would like to achieve or problem that you would like to solve and then apply the What? How? What? How? formula.

THE PHASE OF THE LOTUS... CARING FOR YOUR POWERFUL SELF

Another really dope version of me has emerged.
—Unknown

At first glance, one might not think much of the lotus flower. The plant's colors and symmetry are striking, sure, but beneath the lotus's delicate exterior lies a deeper meaning nearly as old as time. The flower holds great symbolic weight in many Eastern cultures and is considered one of the most sacred plants in the world. In its earliest stages of growth, it is true that at times, the lotus is confused: Why so much mud and muck? The lotus can seem quite overwhelmed by these oppressive conditions, being just a stem with only a few leaves and a tiny flower pod. For the lotus, it seems that the world is all about mud! But at some point, the lotus, in its determination to grow, realizes that there in the dark, it can actually extract nutrients from the very environment that stifles it! Little by little, it uses these nutrients to grow. Slowly it rises and surfaces above the oppressive mud and water, finally freeing itself from the harsh life below. It is then that the lotus reveals its beauty to the world—a symbol of rebirth, resilience, and spiritual enlightenment.

Like the lotus flower, there will come a time in your process of growth when the process of confronting yourself and learning to trust your highest self will finally result in a profound aha! moment, accompanied by the awareness that you will reemerge into the world more congruent! I call this phase of change the phase of the lotus. Although I briefly discussed this phase of the process earlier in the book, I'd like to take the opportunity to dive deeper because frankly, this is the point of it all. Up to this point, I have placed much emphasis on the work that occurs in the first and second phases of transformational change. I am sure you have noticed much overlap in many of the concepts discussed up to this point.

Remember, phase one represents the period of increased awareness. Unwittingly, we begin to notice all of the things that feel wrong or out of place in our lives. The intensity builds over time and we find ourselves in the midst of an existential storm. Because so many can buckle under the pressure of this experience or cling to old ways of surviving, the primary tasks required to move through this space are twofold. First, you must be open to shifting your perspective to one that allows you to see that the storm is simply a revelation that you are operating (or thinking) out of alignment with what truly matters to you. Second, the storm is an invitation to assess where you have gone astray and to reorient yourself on the path towards your valued direction. This path should be one that reflects your values and ultimately, your understanding of G-d.

The second phase of this journey is all about confronting your ego. This is the lower version of self that holds many of the beliefs, rules, and assumptions that are currently shaping how you show up in the world. While many of your beliefs and rules are healthy, others breed self-doubt, fear, and scarcity, and are ultimately obstructing your clarity and ability to believe in the abundance of possibilities that lie ahead of you. These beliefs also have an impact on how you seek, access, and respond to G-d. In order to navigate this phase effectively, you must be willing to tease out the ways of thinking and doing that are currently impairing your ability to move toward your valued direction. Once identified, you must be willing to revise your ways of thinking and doing to support your valued direction. This will require you to create space for your highest self to emerge. This will require you to become spiritually attuned. It will require you to confront fear and scarcity. It will require you to connect to and nurture your inner child, and it will require you to become aware of the ways in which your earlier pain is manifesting in your life. Remember, this phase of growth takes the longest, and while it will be challenging, it can also be the start of something beautiful. I'll say this, I realized that I was navigating out of this phase when I stopped pretending to be anything other than what I was and began to direct all my energy into loving and embracing that woman. It turned out that the "happiness" that I had longed for throughout my life was, in fact, a spirit of peace and calm.

Finally, you enter into the phase of the lotus. Using the words of Akshara Noor, within this phase of harmony and flow, "there are no more maps, no more creeds, no more philosophies." From here on, all direction comes straight from the Divine. The curriculum is being revealed millisecond by millisecond—invisibly, intuitively, spontaneously, and lovingly. This phase is all about maintaining and cultivating that connection with your highest self. This is the phase in which you begin to exist and operate according to your new self-awareness. It is the phase in which you perform, function, build, and create as one with G-d. This is the phase in which you move through time and space differently; you vibrate differently and higher. Hell, you'll even glow!

I was recently speaking to a former client in this phase and as she shared some of the challenges she had faced in the previous days, she explained, "Nikki, I really feel good! I don't have all of the answers. I am still trying to figure out some things, and I have moments of feeling overwhelmed or sad. But it's as if the Universe keeps reminding me that I am okay, and I am! In general, I am happy, I am at peace; I am less reactive! I can't believe that I am finally saying that! Everything just isn't hitting me like it used to!" With respect to her privacy, I will say this—sistah went through it in the years and months leading up to this moment, so to see her beaming with calm made my spirit soar! But as I mentioned, she is and has been doing the work; she pushed through the resistance, the doubt, the fear of grief, and the breakdowns! She has learned how to trust herself and is becoming more aligned in acceptance of herself.

So, the key to existing in this stage is maintenance. I'll be honest, this is an area in which I am living real time, and there is still much to learn. But I'd like to share in the following section some of the things that I am doing to maintain my congruence and connection.

Caring for Your Congruent and Powerful Self

Understand That You Have a Vibrational Frequency

Everything in the human body breaks down to energy! The body itself is composed of different systems, which are made up of organs and tissues. The organs and tissues are made of cells, which are made of molecules, which are made up of atoms and so forth. So, the basic idea of vibrational frequency is that we are not solid matter but energy, and all energy vibrates at a particular frequency. When we reach a high frequency in our personal energy signature, we attract more positive emotions and experiences. Love, for instance, is a very high-frequency emotion. When we emit a low frequency, we drop into an ego-based mindset that can attract negativity, stress, anxiety, and depression into our experiences. The idea is that whatever is happening in your life, which is also energy with its own frequency, it must be vibrating at the same frequency as you are. If your life is fabulous, it's because your frequency is fabulous. If your life is in the doldrums, so too is your frequency. The idea that "everything is energy" is far from "woo"; it's a scientific fact.

But it is important to note that sometimes we fall into a scarcity mindset, believing that we're chronically unlucky. Mostly, however, we are simply dealing with the experiences, situations, and people that we're attracting like a magnet through our own personal vibrational frequencies. Thankfully, through mindfulness and strong intention, we have the power to bring positivity, beauty, happiness, and other joys into our lives. This is also why perspective is so important.

Unfortunately, this basic premise often gets lost and people tend to use their vibrational frequency as a barometer for progress. If you focus on whether you think you are vibrating on a high frequency, you're already missing the point, so I want to be clear in saying that I am not sharing this information so that you can become one of those people who tries to avoid all discomfort in order to maintain a high frequency. If you become this person, you will likely fall prey to the habit of constantly measuring your progress by some arbitrary standard of positivity and skipping the deeper work that understanding vibrational frequency allows you to do. So, I am sharing this because I want to support you in becoming more aware of how to care for yourself when your frequency is interrupted—and it will be interrupted!

A great resource for helping to maintain wellness is Reiki. In short, Reiki is a Japanese technique for stress reduction and relaxation that also promotes healing at the energetic level. It is administered by "laying hands on" or hovering just above the body and is based on the idea that an unseen "life force energy" flows through us, serving as the source of our existence as living beings. If one's "life force energy" is low, then they are more likely to get sick or feel stress; if it is high, they are more capable of becoming and staying happy and healthy.

Healing crystals can be another great addition to your energetic wellness routine. Healing crystals and gemstones have been used for thousands of years by ancient civilizations. The Egyptians, Aztecs, and others incorporated healing stones into jewelry, cosmetics, decorative statues, amulets, and much more—a testament to gemstones' powerful ability to release mental, physical, and spiritual blockages.

Since our bodies have energetic vibrations, we are naturally receptive to the vibrations of gemstones, as they can align our own vibrations with theirs. This energy surges from the crystal to you, which facilitates the free flow of energy throughout the body. This is an area that I am studying more, so if you are also interested in exploring further, here are a few that you can start with.

1. Clear Quartz

Clear quartz is a versatile healing crystal that can be programmed for many different purposes. The clear-colored cleansing crystal has the ability to direct energies and can also amplify and enhance the energy of other gemstones. Place a clear quartz crystal in each corner of a room to remove negative energy.

2. Rose Quartz

Commonly known as the love stone, pale pink rose quartz promotes emotional healing. The powerful healing properties and energies of rose quartz are associated with the heart chakra. The stone can be used for self-love or for maintaining healthy loving relationships with others. It also helps you to open your heart in a compassionate way and allows you to be receptive to giving and receiving.

3. Amethyst

Amethyst is available in many shades of purple, from pale lavender to violet. The healing crystal has deep cleansing properties and can be used for personal protection. When an amethyst crystal is positioned directly onto the body, it can alleviate pain and minimize stress, while also strengthening the immune system.

4. Citrine

Associated with the solar plexus, yellow citrine crystal is often called the money stone. The crystal clears negative energy and enhances prosperity in all areas of your life. Citrine is beneficial for healing of the liver, kidney, or bladder infections, and blood disorders. Carrying a small piece of citrine in your pocket, purse, or handbag can also boost your luck with money.

5. Hematite

Dark gray/black hematite crystal is metallic and helps to deflect negative energy. The powerful crystal has reflective bounce-off qualities that make it perfect for clearing harmful energies and maintaining a positive aura. Hematite is associated with the root chakra and is an excellent grounding stone. It can be used to heal health issues relating to the feet, knees, and legs.

6. Smoky Quartz

Translucent smoky quartz absorbs negative energies from your physical and emotional environment. The crystal is available in a wide variety of smoky shades from brown to gray and black. Smoky quartz is a premium transmuting and anchoring stone that can also be used to enhance the protection around you.

7. Amazonite

This healing crystal promotes harmony and balance, and helps to dispel negative thinking, fears, and worry. The mineral gemstone is associated with the throat chakra and is often used to enhance communication, intellect, creativity, psychic abilities, and intuition.

8. Jade

Jade is a powerful crystal that can attract harmony and abundance. The pale to dark green protective stone guards against misfortune and can be used for self-healing. Jade's positive prosperous energies can help you bring more love and luck into your life.

Again, integrating crystals and gems into your spiritual practice may not be for you, so I encourage you to do your own research. I particularly like to incorporate into my meditation and prayer as a means to amplify my connection.

Revisit Your Valued Direction...Often

If it has yet to become clear, one of the things that you will come to learn is that this process will refine your valued direction. With each aha! moment that you experience in the ego-confrontation phase, you reveal a more authentic version of yourself. With these revelations come inspiration and a sense of "I can take on the world!" So it is important then, to keep your valued direction in the forefront of your thoughts. In other words, within this state of being, you want to make sure that your decisions remain aligned with your valued direction because you are going to be operating from a point of view that truly inspires you. This is where learning how to discern between a good thing and a G-d thing really comes into play.

A good way to stay connected to your valued direction is simply incorporating the following question into your decision making: "Does this way of thinking, being, or doing move me closer to my valued direction, or does it keep me stuck?" You can also start each morning asking, "What can I do today that moves me towards my valued direction?" or "What value can I honor or practice today that moves me towards my valued direction?" If you didn't highlight any of those questions, please do. At the end of the day, I want to dissuade you from allowing your threshold for discomfort to be the framework for your decision-making. The truth is that discomfort is an inherent reality of living. The question is, do you want to make decisions according to the discomfort that keeps you stuck or the discomfort that moves you forward?

Embracing Consistency

It is said that success doesn't come from what you do occasionally, but from what you do consistently.

It is also true that learning to be consistent requires practice and patience. When you begin to experience the sense of ease that comes with experiencing alignment, it is important not to rest on your laurels. Instead, it is time to develop a wellness routine that promotes your consistency. As I mentioned earlier, transformational growth is constantly unfolding, and while you will make major strides, life will give you additional "opportunities" to further refine and develop. Sometimes those "opportunities" will feel like tests, and sometimes that is exactly what they will be. Adhering to the same principles and courses of action that are moving you towards your valued direction is a great way to promote maintenance in this phase. In other words, in addition to doing the transformative work to achieve congruence, you want to continue to do all of the things that you did to allow your highest self to emerge. Creating a wellness routine that promotes your congruence and connection to your highest self and G-d are key. Remember, consistency will always feel like more of an inconvenience when you are just starting out. The brain has not yet been conditioned to associate value with the new actions that you are taking to grow.

Setting and Maintaining Boundaries

I think that on a fundamental level, you and I both understand the importance of maintaining boundaries. Again, if this is an area that you've struggled with, in many cases, it will be the work that you unpack in phase two. In other words, the fear behind setting or maintaining boundaries should be worked out by this phase. It's not that you won't get moments of agh!, but you just won't feel as compelled to act on the angst.

Even though we are familiar with the importance of boundaries I cannot miss an opportunity to spend some time discussing them from my point of view. A point of view that I often share with my clients understanding that they will reconfigure in a way that makes the most sense to them. The first thing that I'd like to point out here is that there are two categories of boundaries. Boundaries that pertain to how we navigate others are called interpersonal boundaries. Interpersonal boundaries are all directly related to your personal, professional, and familial relationships. These are the boundaries that honor your values, protect your space, and regulate your energetic and emotional output. Setting these boundaries accordingly also optimizes your spiritual connection to the Universe. Remember what I said earlier in this book. Your ability to prioritize yourself first in a thoughtful and positively intention-oriented manner is not an act of selfishness, but an act of service and awareness of your function as an instrument to do G-d's work.

Intrapersonal boundaries refer to your relationship with your ego-driven self. As I have explained, the ego is the mind's identity of our own construction, an identity of "I." It is our connection to the world and everything in it. If we take all of the beliefs of what we are—beliefs about our personalities, talents, and abilities—we have the structure of our egos. Like the parts that compose our inner children, there is no getting rid of it; and while our highest selves are important, our egos are also a necessary part of our existence.

So, the goal of setting boundaries with yourself is all about compassionately keeping your ego in check. If I could paint a picture, it would depict a car with your highest self in the driver's seat, your ego in the passenger seat, and your inner child in the back seat, all happily driving towards your valued direction!

I begin with a simple exercise with my clients. I ask them to look in the mirror every morning after brushing their teeth and say to themselves, either aloud or inside, "Today, I come from my Higher Self, not from my ego." It's like reprogramming your thought process. I encourage my clients to say this to themselves at least five times combined with deep breathing.

Honor Your Body

Believe it or not, what you put in your body directly affects your mood, sleep, and vibrational energy. Foods such as raw fruits and veggies offer nourishment for our minds and bodies and allow us to perform at our most optimal levels. If you want to feel more vibrant, try incorporating more fresh, ripe fruits and vegetables into your diet. Meat, dairy, and processed foods take a long time to digest and rob our bodies of vital energy.

Fruits and veggies digest quickly, and give our bodies the fuel they need to function properly. Now, I am not suggesting that you close this book and sign up for your next diet, nor am I promoting veganism or some sort of fast. In fact, I'd like to ask you to let go of the idea of dieting all together. Diets are an excellent way to deprive you of your intuitive connection to your body. The inability to maintain your diet of choice promotes a mindset of defeat that can echo your language of failure. If you're good at dieting, it can create a false sense of authority, purity, and control. While I have not provided an in-depth reflection on the prevalence of eating disorders amongst Black women (I'll save that for another book!), I will say that we are not removed from this struggle. Health can be achieved at every size and we must make certain not to fall into the traps that promote one body ideal as the image of success, beauty, and wellness.

If you want to make a shift in your relationship with food, if you want to transition to veganism or vegetarianism because it will better align with your values and health goals, then I recommend working with a clinician like myself who has a clinical specialty in treating disordered eating and negative body image, as well as a registered dietitian also experienced in successfully working with individuals who struggle with disordered eating. The proper guidance will greatly contribute to a more optimal relationship with food and your body.

But honoring your body isn't just limited to what you put in it. It also encompasses regular exercise and rest. For me, there is nothing like that after-workout euphoria that makes me feel like I can do and be anything! There was a time in my life in which I hated exercise. It felt more like a chore, and I felt like my body was a problem to be fixed. However, I started to notice similarities in the mindset I was operating in to navigate my own change process and fitness routine. I was lazy, negative, and inconsistent! When I began to shift my mindset through consistently showing up to the gym to challenge myself, my relationship to exercise and my body started to shift as well. Now, I exercise because I want to be in the best mental, spiritual, and physical shape that I can be to do the work that I am being called to do.

Rest is just as important! As someone with a long history of intense depressive episodes, I had to learn that working myself into a state of tired, or worse, exhaustion were major triggers. As I have explained to my clients. If you are someone who struggles with depression, your brain doesn't necessarily know the somatic difference between sadness and tired; because, in many ways, it feels the same. So, when I would find myself completely tired from all of the work that came with running my business and family, it was as if the walls of my emotional immune system came tumbling down. My brain would yell, "queue the other symptoms!" and just like that, I was down for the count. So, If you have struggled with depression, anxiety, PTSD and eating disorder, etc. It is perfectly okay to care for yourself accordingly. If you were a survivor of cancer, I am pretty sure you would take all of the proper precautions to keep that cancer in remission. Your mental health is no different.

There are so many things that I can share and say about this phase, but I think that it's time to let you experience it for yourself! While you may find yourself revisiting some storms here and there, remember the function, shift your perspective, and receive the invitation to reorient yourself and lean in. You'll notice yourself cycling through the phases with more authority and confidence in knowing that you are becoming a more enlightened and powerful woman.

Reflection Questions:

- What have been your major takeaways from this book?

FINAL THOUGHTS...
A CALL TO ACTION

Heaven bestows, yet we must receive. For what has happened, I give thanks. For what is happening, I send praise. For what is to happen, I have faith.
—Unknown

If you are reading these words, you have made it through the book. My hope is that you have found these perspectives to be helpful affirmations of what has already existed within your beautiful spirit. As you can see, so much of the work is interwoven. While you may not be unburdened by all of your beliefs after reading this book, I hope that I have successfully conveyed the value of seeking support. By no means, Sis, do you have to walk this path absent of guidance and support. But remember, everyone's process will be their own. You will struggle, you will question, and you will stumble. This doesn't mean that you are doing it wrong; it simply means that you are fighting for you, so fight with all of your heart and all of your hope!

With that said, I must confess that I am very much a graduating student from the school of less is more. Rather than sharing more anecdotes and additional instructions, I'd like to use my final words as a call to action. As I have said, the ultimate goal of transformation is to contribute to the world's advancement in your own unique way. As we let our own light shine, we unconsciously give others permission to do the same. Critically, however, we must adhere to three rules of thumb:

1. We cannot truly experience the depth and breadth of this change with one foot in the bullshit. Sorry that I couldn't be more eloquent here.

2. Change is uncomfortable. The more you resist and avoid the discomfort the more you will revert back to old behaviors and delay your growth.

3. Without action, even the most evolved and transformed person is like a new car without an engine: It looks great, but it doesn't go anywhere.

Without action, no amount of therapy, meditation, or prayer will bring about the transformation that you seek. So, as you close this final chapter, consider what actions you need to take next. I hope you have enjoyed the digital companion journal, stay connected via Instagram, visit me at www.solcenteredlife.com to learn about our amazing programs and resources, purchase the Purposeful Perspectives: Self-Mastery card deck and join The Purposeful Woman group on Facebook!

If our paths never cross, know that I, too, am a fellow traveler in pursuit of my power, and I am wishing you all the best. Peace and love, sis!

ACKNOWLEDGMENTS

I have to take a moment to express my deep and heartfelt gratitude to Shannon (my sister), Mercedes, Porscher, Katrina, and my momma and daddy! Your words of encouragement, guidance, and support through this process have been nothing short of comforting. To my right-hand Mary, you are a true gift and blessing. Jennifer, thank you for being a kick-ass book coach that consistently held space for me to be a complete mess throughout this process.

I am also deeply grateful that The Source of all life deemed me worthy of this journey. I will continue to ready myself for the work to come.

RESOURCES

Values List

Abundance	Community	Flexibility
Acceptance	Commitment	Friendships
Accountability	Compassion	Freedom
Achievement	Consistency	Fun
Adventure	Contribution	Generosity
Advocacy	Cooperation	Grace
Ambition	Creativity	Growth
Appreciation	Credibility	Happiness
Attractiveness	Curiosity	Health
Autonomy	Daring	Honesty
Balance	Decisiveness	Humility
Being the Best	Dedication	Humor
Benevolence	Dependability	Inclusiveness
Boldness	Diversity	Independence
Brilliance	Empathy	Individuality
Calmness	Encouragement	Innovation
Caring	Enthusiasm	Inspiration
Challenge	Ethics	Intelligence
Charity	Excellence	Intuition
Cheerfulness	Expressiveness	Joy
Cleverness	Fairness	Kindness
Collaboration	Family	Knowledge

Leadership

Learning

Love

Loyalty

Making a
  Difference

Mindfulness

Motivation

Optimism

Open-Mindedness

Originality

Passion

Performance

Personal

Development

Peace

Perfection

Playfulness

Popularity

Power

Preparedness

Proactivity

Proactive

Professionalism

Punctuality

Quality

Recognition

Relationships

Reliability

Resilience

Resourcefulness

Responsibility

Responsiveness

Risk Taking

Safety/Security

Self-Control

Selflessness

Service

Simplicity

Spirituality

Stability

Success

Teamwork

Thankfulness

Thoughtfulness

Traditionalism

Trustworthiness

Understanding

Uniqueness

Usefulness

Versatility

Vision

Warmth

Wealth

Well-Being

Wisdom

Zeal

List of Feeling Words

Pleasant Feelings

OPEN

understanding

confident

reliable

easy

amazed

free

sympathetic

interested

satisfied

receptive

accepting

kind

HAPPY

great

joyous

lucky

fortunate

delighted

overjoyed

gleeful

thankful

important

festive

ecstatic

glad

cheerful

elated

jubilant

ALIVE

playful

courageous

energetic

liberated

optimistic

impulsive

free

animated

spirited

thrilled

wonderful

GOOD

calm

peaceful

at ease

comfortable

pleased

encouraged

clever

surprised

content

quiet

certain

relaxed

serene

reassured

LOVE

loving

considerate

affectionate

sensitive

tender

devoted

attracted

passionate

admiration

warm

touched

close

comforted

loved

INTERESTED

concerned

affected

fascinated

intrigued

absorbed

inquisitive

engrossed

curious

drawn toward

POSITIVE

eager

keen

earnest

intent

inspired

determined

excited

enthusiastic

bold

brave

daring

optimistic

STRONG

impulsive

free

sure

certain

rebellious

unique

dynamic

tenacious

hardy

secure

confident

challenged

Unpleasant Feelings

ANGRY

irritated

enraged

hostile

insulting

annoyed

upset

hateful

offensive

bitter

aggressive

resentful

inflamed

provoked

incensed

infuriated

cross

worked up

boiling

fuming

DEPRESSED

lousy

disappointed

discouraged

ashamed

powerless

diminished

guilty

dissatisfied

miserable

detestable

repugnant

despicable

disgusting

abominable

terrible

in despair

sulky

bad

CONFUSED

upset

doubtful

uncertain

indecisive

perplexed

embarrassed

hesitant

shy

stupefied

disillusioned

unbelieving

skeptical

distrustful

misgiving

lost

unsure

uneasy

pessimistic

tense

HELPLESS

incapable

alone

paralyzed

fatigued

useless

inferior

vulnerable

empty

forced

hesitant

despair

frustrated

distressed

woeful

pathetic

tragic

in a stew

dominated

INDIFFERENT

insensitive

dull

nonchalant

neutral

reserved

weary

bored

preoccupied

cold

disinterested

lifeless

AFRAID

fearful

terrified

suspicious

anxious

alarmed

panic

nervous

scared

worried

frightened

timid

shaky

restless

doubtful

threatened

cowardly

quaking

wary

HURT

crushed

tormented

deprived

pained

tortured

dejected

rejected

injured

offended

afflicted

aching

victimized

heartbroken

agonized

appalled

humiliated

wronged

alienated

SAD

tearful

sorrowful

pained

grief

anguish

desolate

desperate

pessimistic

unhappy

lonely

grieved

mournful

dismayed

ABOUT THE AUTHOR

Nichomi Higgins, also known as "Nikki," is a well-respected leadership coach, professor of psychology at Pepperdine University, spiritual mentor, and practicing psychotherapist. As a passionate champion for the mental and spiritual well-being of professional women of color, Nichomi is determined to create safe spaces that allow powerful women to redefine what it means to be exceptional. She has had the good fortune to have a rich and varied life, not free from adversity, but shaped by it.

Over the last decade, Nichomi's work with high achieving professional women in business and leadership has been fueled by her 15+ years of clinical and leadership experience, as well as her core values—grace, vision, sisterhood, spirituality, sustainability, and abundance. These values greatly influence her ability to connect to her clients on a more meaningful level that serves as a catalyst for dynamic shifts in mindset and growth.

Furthermore, Nichomi is one of the few professionals of color honing an extensive background in treating eating disorders and negative body image amongst women of color. In addition to eating disorder treatment, her clinical specialties include depression, anxiety, and religious trauma. Mrs. Higgins is not only a champion of wellness amongst professional women, but she is also a noted practitioner. She has repeatedly served as a guest expert on the *Dr. Phil* show, a nationally broadcasted daytime talk series viewed by millions. Nichomi values creating platforms that inspire and empower women to connect to their divine authority in order to create from the best versions of themselves. This is why in 2021, she will be launching the SolCentered Life Academy for women of color who desire to amplify their light as powerful and purpose-driven life coaches.

When Nichomi is not operating in service to others, she absolutely loves spending time with her family and friends, dancing, goofing around, and staring at trees.

Don't Forget Your
Purposeful Perspectives
Self-Mastery Deck!

CPSIA information can be obtained
at www.ICGtesting.com
Printed in the USA
BVHW040723210621
609824BV00033B/2474/J

9 781736 025819